PENGUIN

BAMBER GASCOIGNE'S CHALLENGING QUIZ BOOK

BAMBER GASCOIGNE is best known as the quizmaster for twenty-five years of *University Challenge*, which he hosted from its launch in 1962. But the central part of his professional life has been as an author, of books and television documentaries.

He has published three novels and several children's books, illustrated by his wife, Christina, but most of his books have been on widely ranging historical subjects. A particular interest has been the history of prints, resulting in *Milestones in Colour Printing* and *How to Identify Prints*, now a standard text-book in colleges and museums. His *Encyclopedia of Britain* covers all the best-known aspects of British history and culture.

Since 1994 he has been writing a digital history of the world for the internet. It went online in 2001 as www.historyworld.net and in 2002 won the *New Statesman* New Media award as Britain's best educational website. In 2007 he launched a related site, at www.timesearch.info, using timelines as a way of searching the internet.

He and his wife have lived near the Thames in Richmond since 1967.

The answers to the questions on the back cover can be found on pages 319, 231, 247 (twice), 300 and 380.

BAMBER GASCOIGNE

Bamber Gascoigne's Challenging Quiz Book

ALLEN LANE
an imprint of
PENGUIN BOOKS

PENGUIN BOOKS

Published by the Penguin Group
Penguin Books Ltd, 80 Strand, London WC2R 0RL, England
Penguin Group (USA) Inc., 375 Hudson Street, New York, New York 10014, USA
Penguin Group (Canada), 90 Eglinton Avenue East, Suite 700,
Toronto, Ontario, Canada M4P 2Y3
(a division of Pearson Penguin Canada Inc.)
Penguin Ireland, 25 St Stephen's Green, Dublin 2, Ireland
(a division of Penguin Books Ltd)
Penguin Group (Australia), 250 Camberwell Road,
Camberwell, Victoria 3124, Australia
(a division of Pearson Australia Group Pty Ltd)
Penguin Books India Pvt Ltd, 11 Community Centre,
Panchsheel Park, New Delhi – 110 017, India
Penguin Group (NZ), 67 Apollo Drive, Rosedale, North Shore 0632, New Zealand
(a division of Pearson New Zealand Ltd)
Penguin Books (South Africa) (Pty) Ltd, 24 Sturdee Avenue, Rosebank,
Johannesburg 2196, South Africa

Penguin Books Ltd, Registered Offices: 80 Strand, London WC2R 0RL, England

www.penguin.com

First published 2007
1

Typeset by Palimpsest Book Production Limited,
Grangemouth, Stirlingshire
Printed in England by Clays Ltd, St Ives plc

ISBN: 978-0-141-03470-6

To my colleagues in the great adventure
of HistoryWorld and TimeSearch

Preface

In several ways this book is a direct result of *University Challenge*. In the most obvious sense, my interest in general knowledge derives from days, weeks, months with my nose in encyclopedias – even years, come to think of it. I used to spend a day reading round the questions before each trip to Manchester to record two programmes. In twenty-five years there were about 500 recording days. If I am allowed a five-day week and four weeks' holiday a year, that works out at two years and a month pottering around among random scraps of information.

So I have had a necessary interest in facts. But the link with *University Challenge* goes deeper. The experience of asking so many questions, to intelligent and highly competitive students, convinced me that there is a broadly definable territory that almost deserves capitals and can be called General Knowledge. It consists of all the information that for many people will ring at least a faint bell, however far away in the back of the mind.

If I asked the students a difficult question that nevertheless fell within this territory, there would always be one or two who would look distraught, clasp their hands to their foreheads, sit up very straight, sway back and forth – all symptoms expressing 'surely, surely, surely I know that?' And then, when I gave the answer, there would be an exhalation, a gentle collapse, a smile and the hint of a nod, as if to say, 'yes, of course!'

If a question was way outside the territory, the reaction would be very different – a look of startled bewilderment to be followed, when the unheard-of answer came, by the nearest one can get to expressing outrage in silence.

So what lies within the boundaries of general knowledge? The information inside has earned its place for good reason – most often because it is genuinely important (significant moments or famous people in politics, war, literature, art, entertainment), or because it has always had tabloid appeal (Jack the Ripper, the death of a suffragette in the Derby, the sinking of the *Titanic*), or because a character is horrible (Scrooge) or endearing (Mr Pooter) or both (Toad), or because a quotation has tickled the public's fancy – 'mad, bad and dangerous to know' said of Byron, or more recently, 'he would, wouldn't he?' in the Profumo case, and Mrs Thatcher's glowing tribute to her deputy, William Whitelaw: 'Every prime minister needs a Willie.'

The territory is, of course, different in different contexts. There is international and national and local general knowledge. But in each case the borders are self-perpetuating. It is within them that journalists or speech-writers look for analogies and metaphors, because they know that their audience will meet them halfway. It is here that people setting quizzes instinctively seek out their questions, in the confidence that they are likely to be answered. And the more the facts within get repeated, the more unfamiliar become those lying outside – exactly as bestselling authors, by their dominance of the bookshop windows and the column inches, move steadily further away from the competition.

This belief in the reality of General Knowledge prompted a book that I wrote about fifteen years ago. Called *Encyclopedia of Britain*, it was an attempt to deal with the best-known details of every aspect of life in this country, whether in politics or art, science or religion, football or fashion or food. I asked a sample selection of people what they considered the leading names or places or events in each field. A clear consensus seemed to emerge and I followed it – justified, I think, by the fact that very few readers have ever complained of specific omissions.

This quiz book continues the theme. It is linked to two large general-knowledge websites on which I have spent all my time for the past ten years. I moved into digital information after being bowled over by the first serious CD-ROM that came my way (it contained, described, compared and set in context all the paintings in London's National Gallery). It made me decide that I must write for this extraordinary new medium, and the first topic that occurred to me was a large one – no less than a narrative encyclopedia of world history in interactive form. This is now online under the title *HistoryWorld* (at www.historyworld.net). From it, there has recently emerged an offspring, *TimeSearch* (at www.timesearch.info), which uses 10,000 events from world history as a way of searching the internet for historical content.

Both these projects operate within the territory of General Knowledge, and the answer to each of the 2000 questions in this book can be found in them (indeed the date given within each question or answer will lead you to more information on the subject if you go to that year in *TimeSearch* and follow the links).

I hope that a fair number of the questions will ring a bell with you. They are often not as hard as they may seem. Like the bonus questions in *University Challenge*, each set is linked by a common theme which can serve also as a clue. The vignettes illustrating the pages have been selected to relate in a general way to that set of questions, and the precise underlying themes are given at the head of each set of answers.

The skilful quiz player wins not necessarily by knowing the answers but by having sufficient knowledge to make informed guesses. And the skilful quiz question offers hints as to the range within which those guesses should be made. I hope you will find helpful hints in the pages that follow.

Questions

I

1. Which nine-year-old boy was profoundly inspired by the beauty of which eight-year-old girl, in thirteenth-century Florence?

2. Which couple popularized in England in the 1840s the custom of a family Christmas tree?

3. Who visited whom in southern Turkey in 41 BC, arriving in a golden barge?

4. Which film stars married each other for the second time in 1975?

5. Which pair of lovers formed the title of the early-twentieth-century US musical that included the song 'He Done Me Wrong'?

6. Which two English poets went to live in Florence after marrying secretly in the 1840s?

7. In which Italian city did Nelson meet Emma?

8. Which couple were played by Faye Dunaway and Warren Beatty in the 1960s?

9. Which Hector fell desperately in love with Harriet, an Irish actress, when he saw her play Ophelia and Juliet in Paris in the 1820s?

10. Which ill-fated pair of lovers did Chelsea schoolgirls sing about in a new opera in the 1680s?

2

1. For whose coronation did Handel compose *Zadok the Priest*?

2. Who, most notably, was down and out in Paris and London in the 1930s?

3. Who led the guerrilla movement EOKA, fighting for Cyprus's independence from Britain and union with Greece?

4. Which engineer called his first locomotive the *Blucher*, and ran it at the Killingworth colliery, north of Newcastle?

5. Which little-known politician did President de Gaulle appoint in the early 1960s as France's premier?

6. Who led a disastrous cavalry attack on the Sioux, at the Little Bighorn River?

7. Who began preaching in England in the 1650s, launching a movement that developed into the Society of Friends (the Quakers)?

8. Whose men killed ten French soldiers near Fort Duquesne, in the first violent clash of the French and Indian War?

9. Whose painting *Houses at l'Estaque* is considered a very early example of analytic Cubism?

10. Which English metaphysical poet is the author of *The Temple*, a volume published posthumously and containing almost his entire output?

3

1. What colour was forced upon Hester Prynne, in a Nathaniel Hawthorne novel?

2. What do small things have, according to Arundhati Roy?

3. What was unbearable in the title of a Czech novel published in the 1980s?

4. On this side of what did Scott FitzGerald's characters live, in his first novel?

5. Who has a parrot, in a Julian Barnes title?

6. What did Thomas Pynchon give to gravity?

7. To what did Françoise Sagan say good morning?

8. What was the garden made of, in Ian McEwan's first novel?

9. What was Henderson, according to Saul Bellow?

10. What was pursued in the title of the novel that was Nancy Mitford's first success?

4

1. Which actress, already well known in the provinces, caused a sensation when she appeared at London's Drury Lane in 1782?

2. In which sport was biting forbidden, in the rules adopted in 1838?

3. What was the London mob violently objecting to in the Gordon Riots?

4. Who opened in London a Mother's Clinic for Birth Control, the first of its kind in Britain?

5. The last new German weapon of the Second World War was first seen when it killed three people in Chiswick, in west London, in September 1944. What was it?

6. Which artist, fleeing from the Franco-Prussian War, came to London and became fascinated by the visual effects of fog?

7. Which American Indian princess arrived in London with her husband to publicize the English settlement at Jamestown, Virginia?

8. What name was given to the health crisis caused in London in 1858 by the polluted Thames and the very hot weather?

9. Which French ballerina moved to London to join the Royal Ballet in 1989?

10. Which painter moved from Suffolk to Hampstead, in London, which became one of his favourite subjects?

5

1. What name is given to the wares with thick transparent green glazes developed by Chinese potters in the Song dynasty?

2. Which building began to rise in Istanbul in the early seventeenth century, almost a twin to the nearby Santa Sophia?

3. Which English narrative poem of the fourteenth century tells of the visit of a mysterious knight to the Round Table of King Arthur?

4. What followed blue in the development of Picasso's palette?

5. In what context did Greenwich become the international standard in the 1880s?

6. Which group of dancers, formed by Margaret Kelly, gave their first performances in Paris in the 1930s?

7. Which novelist described the experiences of seventeen-year-old Pinkie in the criminal underworld of Brighton?

8. Which film, directed by Josef von Sternberg, made Marlene Dietrich an international star?

9. Where has *The Green Book* been a political bible in recent decades?

10. Which Dutch designer produced a famous 'Red and Blue Chair', under the influence of the De Stijl movement?

6

1. What familiar element was first added to a clock one Christmas Day by a Dutch physicist, Christiaan Huygens?

2. For what did Italian US immigrant Antonio Meucci file an early patent, though Alexander Graham Bell was the first to achieve a functioning version?

3. What part of a ship, of huge importance in the history of seafaring, was developed by the Chinese in the twelfth or thirteenth century?

4. What was profoundly significant about the photographs taken by William Henry Fox Talbot one summer at his home, Lacock Abbey?

5. What new writing material is traditionally credited to Eumenes II, the king of Pergamum, and derives its name from his kingdom?

6. Of what was the IBM 5150 the first example on the market, launched in the early 1980s?

7. Spectacles of what kind, now familiar, were first commissioned from a lens-grinder by Benjamin Franklin?

8. What did French physician René Laënnec invent, to avoid the embarrassment of pressing his ear against the bodies of his female patients?

9. What invention by Eli Whitney greatly speeded up the process of separating cotton fibres from the seeds?

10. What time-saving device, seen in many modern kitchens, was first demonstrated by Denis Papin in the late seventeenth century?

7

1. Which group of six works was composed by Johann Sebastian Bach for his employer at the court of Köthen?

2. In which British film did six unemployed steel workers try something very different?

3. The siege of which town came to an end when six burghers offered their own lives to save their fellow citizens?

4. What was formed in 1951 by six European nations, six years before they jointly took an even more momentous step?

5. Six comparative versions of what were displayed in six columns by the Greek scholar Origen in his *Hexapla*?

6. What are Luigi Pirandello's six characters in search of?

7. What name is given to the process that has split a single land mass, Pangaea, into our present six continents?

8. Which region, the subject of much controversy, consists of six counties?

9. Which British batsman hit a record six consecutive centuries in first-class cricket in the early twentieth century?

10. Whose first published work, in the mid eighteenth century, was a collection of six string quartets?

8

1. What is linked to Marin County by a golden gate?

2. Who built the box-girder bridge, a radical new design, over the Menai Strait?

3. Into which river were passengers plunged in Scotland's greatest rail disaster?

4. What name is now applied to the new bridge built to replace an old one in Florence in 1345?

5. Which is the world's first custom-built motor-racing track, near Weybridge in Surrey?

6. Who vigorously promoted the new game of contract bridge in the 1920s?

7. What was the title of Thornton Wilder's second novel, with which he achieved worldwide success?

8. In which town, south of Birmingham, did Herbert Austin set up a factory to manufacture cars?

9. A bridge near Beijing, scene of a significant incident between Japanese and Chinese, is known by the name of which foreign visitor?

10. In what sense did security and Tonbridge prove poorly matched in 2006?

9

1. Who sculpted the Pietà in St Peter's, depicting the Virgin Mary holding the dead Christ on her lap?

2. Who was conceived in the Immaculate Conception?

3. By what name is Our Lady of Guadalupe known, signifying her affinity with the local people of Mexico?

4. What was the name of Madonna's second album, which went on to sell millions of copies?

5. Which diptych was commissioned by Richard II, showing himself being presented to the Virgin and Child?

6. Where in France was the first transatlantic radiotelephone message received, transmitted from Arlington in Virginia?

7. In what part of London did the sisters Virginia and Vanessa live in the early years of the twentieth century?

8. The addition of what substance brought extra attention to Chris Ofili's painting *The Holy Virgin*?

9. In the film of which play by Edward Albee did Richard Burton and Elizabeth Taylor star together?

10. In what sense was Virginia Dare the first of her kind?

10

1. Who, on the first day of 1660, had the remains of a turkey for breakfast and began a new project?

2. Who gave Horace his Sabine farm?

3. Which Greek poet worked for thirty years as a civil servant in Alexandria's Irrigation Service?

4. Which Persian poet of the thirteenth century wrote *Bustan* (*Orchard*)?

5. Which two playwrights were born in England in the same year, in the 1560s?

6. Which New Zealand poet called her first collection *The Eye of the Hurricane*?

7. Which poet was expelled from Oxford in the early nineteenth century for circulating a pamphlet entitled *The Necessity of Atheism*?

8. Who was presented to Kublai Khan in Xanadu and later claimed, in his own account, to have made a very good impression?

9. What action did the Japanese novelist Yukio Mishuma carry out, in 1970, in the traditional Samurai manner?

10. Which book caused Ayatollah Khomeini to declare a fatwa against Salman Rushdie?

11

1. Who created, in Daisy Miller, one of the most delightful of his Americans abroad?

2. In which decade did Holland's tulip mania provide the first example of speculative frenzy in a capitalist market?

3. Which US choreographer joined with Mikhail Baryshnikov in setting up the White Oak Dance Project?

4. Which politician launched a campaign with the cynical slogan: 'Let a hundred flowers bloom'?

5. Brooklyn shopkeepers Morris and Rose Michtom had a huge success with the cuddly doll they named after Theodore Roosevelt. What did they call it?

6. Which US poet's first collection was *Tulips and Chimneys* – or, as he might have preferred it, *tulips and chimneys*?

7. Which nine-year-old created in *The Young Visiters* her own vision of high society and adult romance?

8. An extract from which plant did Socrates drink after being convicted of impiety and corrupting Athenian youth in 399 BC?

9. Whose first and extremely influential collection of poems was *Les Fleurs du mal* (*The Flowers of Evil*)?

10. After defeat in which battle did Charles II have to make his escape by hiding in an oak tree?

12

1. What is the name of the pig which maintains ruthless control of a farm after getting rid of Mr Jones?

2. To celebrate what were about 9000 large animals killed, over a period of 100 days in AD 80?

3. In what surprising place did Louis XVI see a sheep, a cock and a duck in the 1780s, observing them through his telescope?

4. Which large animal, requiring plenty of water, lived 7000 years ago in the region of the present-day Sahara?

5. Caravans of which animals used the 25,000 miles of roads in the Inca empire?

6. Of what real-life show was Jumbo the star attraction?

7. At which institute was Dolly the Sheep cloned?

8. Which tar pit in Los Angeles preserves fossils of mammoths, mastodons and sabre-toothed cats?

9. A tiny pregnant female, captured in Syria in the 1930s, is the ancestor of every children's pet of her kind around the world – what kind of pet?

10. What historically significant animal was discovered in Mongolia by Nikolai Przewalski?

13

1. What species of human was the boy who died at Nariokotome more than a million years ago?

2. Which place in Palestine is widely regarded as having been civilization's first town?

3. In which century was Pompeii discovered by archaeologists?

4. Which epic is known in its complete form only from clay tablets discovered in the Library of Ashurbanipal in Nineveh?

5. Where did the British archaeologist Leonard Woolley discover a royal cemetery more than 4000 years old?

6. Which was the first cereal to be cultivated by humans?

7. Which animal was the first to be domesticated as a source of food, according to the archaeological record?

8. In which island country is the Jomon culture the beginning of the neolithic era?

9. What name has been given to the circle of oak posts discovered in 1998 in Norfolk at low tide?

10. Which archaeological site in Anatolia is the most extensive surviving example of a neolithic town?

14

1. Who designed a geodesic dome for the US pavilion at Expo '67?

2. Who designed a spectacular setting for the first of the Nazi Party's annual Nuremberg rallies?

3. Which US architect designed the City Edge project in Berlin, building it up from startlingly fragmented forms?

4. What high-profile competition was won in 1957 by Jørn Utzon?

5. Who won the competition to construct a dome above Florence's cathedral?

6. Of what festival was the Skylon a central feature?

7. Who won the competition to design a new cathedral for Coventry after the Second World War?

8. For which new capital city was Oscar Niemeyer appointed chief architect?

9. Which Spanish architect died in the 1920s after being hit by a tram?

10. Which Finnish architect won the competition in the early twentieth century to build Helsinki's railway station?

15

1. Where was Shi Huangdi buried, attended by a large army?

2. Who derived his name from the frozen river on which he defeated a Swedish army?

3. What river came to be seen as a turning point, after Julius Caesar took his army across it?

4. Which national army changed sides when it suddenly attacked the Japanese in the Second World War?

5. What name was given to England's first professional army, formed by Thomas Fairfax and Oliver Cromwell?

6. Which famous French author served in Napoleon's army during the invasion of Russia?

7. What do the initials ANZAC stand for?

8. Which nation's army was the first to adopt a breech-loading rifle, the 'needle gun', developed in the mid nineteenth century by Johann Nikolaus von Dreyse?

9. Which artist served in the First World War with the Royal Army Medical Corps and found a wealth of material?

10. Which army in Australia produced an ambitious and very early film called *Soldiers of the Cross*?

16

1. What supposed new discovery by the astronomer John Herschel was reported by *The New York Sun* as a hoax story to boost sales?

2. Which wealthy US astronomer built an observatory at Mars Hill in Flagstaff, Arizona?

3. What proposal was put forward by Bertil Lindblad in the 1920s to explain the irregular movement of stars?

4. Which Polish astronomer published a book suggesting that the earth moves round the sun?

5. In which island did Captain Cook observe the transit of Venus?

6. Which nebula, still visible and named after a sign of the zodiac, derives from the explosion of a supernova observed in the eleventh century by the Chinese?

7. By which year did President Kennedy declare that the USA would have put a man on the moon and brought him safely back?

8. Which comet is depicted in the Bayeux Tapestry?

9. What was the name of the series of spacecraft of which the first, in 1959, passed the moon and went into orbit round the sun?

10. Which nebula did Edwin Hubble prove was too far away to be in our galaxy, and thus had to be itself a galaxy?

17

1. Where in north London was the garden in which a nightingale inspired John Keats?

2. Who was the star of Ridley Scott's film *Gladiator*?

3. What nickname was given to the first communications satellite, launched from Cape Canaveral in 1965?

4. Who was the author of *The Raven and Other Poems*?

5. What bird features in the title of D. H. Lawrence's first novel?

6. Who was given a new and massively influential idea when he ate frozen fish in the Arctic?

7. In which Asian city were homing pigeons first used as postmen, in the eleventh century?

8. Which play by Maurice Maeterlinck was directed by Stanislavsky in 1908?

9. Which Irish author's first novel was *At Swim-Two-Birds*?

10. Which Austrian zoologist demonstrated that young geese will imprint on human beings?

18

1. What name is given to the two wars that began when Covenanters seized control of Edinburgh in 1639?

2. Whose calculation that creation began on Sunday, 23 October 4004 BC was widely accepted for many years?

3. What name is given to the new theology developed by Catholic bishops in Latin America?

4. Which US poet published her first collection of poems in 1946 under the title *North and South*.

5. In which Scottish town did Archbishop David Beaton burn George Wishart as a Protestant heretic?

6. Who painted a magnificent series of frescoes for the prince bishop's residence in Würzburg?

7. In which fractious British colony did Bishop Abel Muzorewa win the first multiracial elections in 1979?

8. Who was the first president of Cyprus as an independent nation?

9. Which missionary reached Canterbury in AD 597 and became the first archbishop of the city?

10. What was the name of the prime minister of Grenada whose execution in 1983 caused President Reagan to send in the marines?

19

1. On which Greek island was the Minoan city of Akrotiri entombed and preserved by a volcanic eruption?

2. Who took hostage an entire theatre audience, resulting in more than 150 deaths?

3. What worldwide disaster, just after the First World War, killed more people than had been killed in the war?

4. Which city was reached and plundered by Celtic tribes in 390 BC?

5. From what company's plant did toxic gas escape in Bhopal, with devastating results?

6. Which book by Voltaire was inspired by a disastrous earthquake in Lisbon?

7. At which US college were thirty-two students and teachers killed by a gunman in the worst ever campus massacre?

8. Which Australian city was devastated by Cyclone Tracy one Christmas Day?

9. What made its first appearance in China in 1346 and reached Europe two years later?

10. On which Indonesian island did a volcano erupt in 1883 and cause a massive tsunami?

20

1. In which theatre did George Devine establish the English Stage Company?

2. With whom did Ken Fletcher achieve the grand slam in mixed doubles?

3. In what sense was Sandra Day O'Connor a significant 'first' in the USA?

4. Who engages in courtship in early New England in the title of a poem by Longfellow?

5. In what kind of building did the delegates of France's Third Estate swear a famous oath?

6. Who became court painter to the king of Spain in the 1620s and held the post until his death thirty-seven years later?

7. In what building did Robert E. Lee surrender to Ulysses S. Grant?

8. Which battle was fought on St Crispin's Day?

9. Which annual French literary prize was established in the will of one of two literary brothers?

10. What type of love is celebrated in the poetry of the troubadours of Provence?

21

1. Which author's novel, from the 1830s, combines in its title red and black?

2. Which nation's armies suffered three defeats in a single 'black week' in the 1890s?

3. Who, with his new group of seven, scored his first major success with *Black Bottom Stomp*?

4. What was the Dutch scientist Anton van Leeuwenhoek the first to observe in blood?

5. Who was sentenced to death by the Blacks in the early fourteenth century and never returned to his native Florence?

6. What was established as a direct result of the horrors seen on the battlefield of Solferino?

7. Which artist exhibited *Black Square* in Petrograd, in the final Futurist exhibition?

8. Which rebellion in Winnipeg prompted the creation of Manitoba as a province of Canada?

9. Which US choreographer formed his first company of dancers at Black Mountain College in North Carolina?

10. Which former Italian prime minister was abducted and assassinated by the Red Brigades?

22

1. What was stolen by Edward I and then, exactly 700 years later, was returned to the scene of the crime?

2. Who wrote an early and passionate feminist work entitled *A Vindication of the Rights of Woman*?

3. What name is given to the revolution in which human communities began to cultivate crops and domesticate animals?

4. Who is the only British prime minister to have moved from opposition to office on four separate occasions?

5. What method of printing was discovered by Alois Senefelder?

6. Which riots in New York in 1969 prompted a campaign for gay and lesbian rights?

7. How was the first Christian martyr killed?

8. Which British explorer was the first to reach the Victoria Falls?

9. Where does the dramatic finale of Thomas Hardy's *Tess of the D'Urbervilles* take place?

10. What was the name of the studio, set up by Mack Sennett in California, that became famous for its knockabout farces?

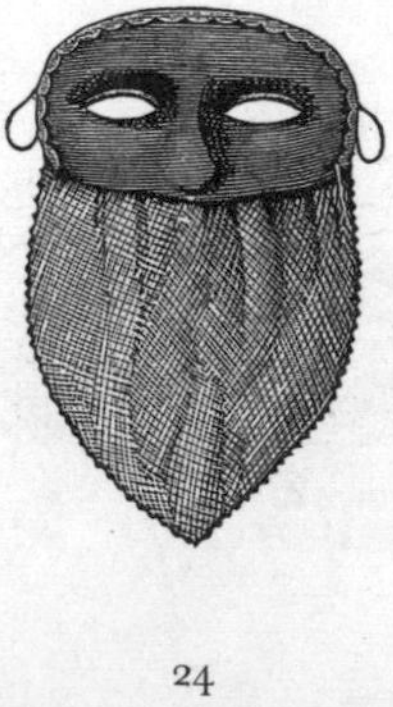

23

1. What is the title of Horace Walpole's very early example of a Gothic novel?

2. Whose novel *The Castle* was published posthumously?

3. The earliest known example of what was held at Rhys ap Gruffydd's court in Cardigan Castle?

4. Who built numerous castles in Wales, including Harlech and Conwy?

5. In which castle was Mary, Queen of Scots, beheaded?

6. Which opera by Béla Bartók was first staged in Budapest at the end of the First World War?

7. Which great crusader castle, still known by its Norman French name, was built by the Knights of St John in the twelfth century?

8. What name was given to the fortified positions hastily built along the south coast of Britain when Napoleon was gathering a fleet to invade?

9. Which castle, adapted to be a high-security prison, received 140 Polish officers as its first inmates?

10. What rare word is used to describe an event in the castle at Prague at the start of the Thirty Years War?

24

1. A club specializing in what game held the first lawn-tennis championship, in the 1870s?

2. In what game is Pudge Heffelfinger considered the first pro, from the day he accepted $500 to play for the Allegheny Athletic Association?

3. Jack Broughton opened an academy in London in the 1740s to teach what he called 'that wholly British art' – the art of what?

4. Veterans of what kind formed the National Rifle Association in the USA, to promote marksmanship?

5. Which game originated in the ancient Persian empire, probably as part of military training?

6. For what sport did the New Yorker Alexander Cartwright devise in the 1840s a set of rules that became the basis of the modern game?

7. What famous trophy derives from Australia's victory in the second Test match, in London in 1882?

8. In what Japanese port is Sukune traditionally held to have won the first competition, in the first century BC?

9. Which city in Ohio fielded the first baseball team composed entirely of professionals, which won every match that year?

10. In what sport was the first competitive event held in the 1890s, over a distance of seventy-eight miles from Paris to Rouen?

25

1. Where did US explorer Richard E. Byrd make a pioneering flight with two companions in the 1920s?

2. Whose first prototype made its test flight at the start of the twentieth century over Lake Constance, and was soon reaching speeds of about 20 mph?

3. Of what was the He-178 the first in the air, with a test flight lasting five minutes?

4. Who set up in Seattle his own Aero Product company, with significant benefits for the city's future prosperity?

5. In which country did young officers led by Flight Lieutenant Jerry Rawlings take power in a coup?

6. Who incautiously flew a kite into a thunder cloud to demonstrate the nature of electricity?

7. From an airport near which French city did the superjumbo Airbus A380 make its first test flight?

8. Which totally unexpected visitor arrived at Floors Farm, south of Glasgow, during the Second World War?

9. Which flying ace shot down twenty-two Allied aircraft in the First World War and subsequently had a notorious political career?

10. Which English aviator made a nineteen-day solo flight from Croydon, near London, to Darwin in Australia?

26

1. What four words complete the title of Benjamin Spock's *Common Sense Book of . . .*?

2. Who published in the sixteenth century *I Quattro Libri dell'Architettura* (*The Four Books of Architecture*), including his influential designs for villas?

3. Saadiah Gaon's *Book of Beliefs and Opinions* is a seminal philosophical work linked with which religion?

4. Which US lexicographer wrote a *Spelling Book* for American children that sold more than 60 million copies?

5. In which country was double-entry book-keeping developed during the late medieval period?

6. Which influential feminist novel by Doris Lessing was published in 1962?

7. All books of what kind were burnt in China on the orders of the Qin dictator Shi Huangdi?

8. Which book did Joseph Smith transcribe from some miraculously discovered holy tablets?

9. What title did Edward Lear give to the book in which he published limericks illustrated with his own cartoons?

10. What is the usual title in English of the book written by Sei Shōnagon, a lady-in-waiting to the Japanese empress?

27

1. The demolition of the old London Bridge put an end to what famous London tradition?

2. What game did the Canadian athlete James Naismith devise to keep his students active indoors in winter?

3. Which Swiss scientist put forward the theory, in his 1836 *Study on Glaciers*, that there had been a fairly recent ice age in Europe?

4. By what nickname did Frederick V of Bohemia become known, because his reign lasted only from one November to the next?

5. Which Ravel score was used by the gold medallists in the ice-dancing event at the Sarajevo Winter Olympics?

6. What name has been given to the last period of the Callaghan government in Britain, because of the number of strikes?

7. Who is the owner of Manderley, in *Rebecca*?

8. Which philosopher caught a fatal chill after returning home in midwinter from a pre-dawn lesson given to Queen Christina of Sweden?

9. Who was assassinated in Mexico City by a blow from an ice-axe?

10. Which palace in which city was stormed in the conclusive moment of victory for the Bolsheviks?

28

1. What did the Romans construct to bring water to the city of Nîmes?

2. Which Mexican people established their capital city at Tula?

3. The fall of which city to Ferdinand and Isabella completed the Christian reconquest of Spain?

4. Which great city was destroyed by the Assyrian king Sennacherib in the seventh century BC?

5. In which musical film did Gene Kelly, Frank Sinatra and Jules Munshin play three US sailors on shore leave?

6. Which city, encroached on by the jungle, was reached and revealed by the US archaeologist Hiram Bingham?

7. Of which civilization was Harappa one of the main cities?

8. Which city has developed from Brigham Young's selection of the site as suitable for settlement?

9. What new kind of city was Letchworth, based on the theories of Ebenezer Howard?

10. Which choreographer founded the New York City Ballet?

29

1. Which singer did Lee De Forest use for his novelty event, a live broadcast from the Metropolitan Opera House in 1910?

2. Which word was coined by Claude Chappe in the late eighteenth century to describe his new system of hilltop signalling?

3. Which new meat product, with a profitable future, was developed in the 1930s by the Hormel company of Austin, Minnesota?

4. Which nation was new in 1918 but lasted only seventy-five years?

5. Which game was first played in India, in the sixth century, before making its way west to Persia?

6. What new system seemed to have cost the British eleven days in 1752?

7. What made the autobiography of Olaudah Equiano unusual, and thus of particular interest?

8. Who published his design for an improved stove, in his 1744 *Account of the New Invented Pennsylvania Fire Place*?

9. What instant commodity was developed in Chicago by the Japanese-American chemist Satori Kato, in the early twentieth century?

10. Who introduced a new fashion when he painted with Renoir in the open air at La Grenouillère?

30

1. What was the title of the film with which Quentin Tarantino made his debut as a director?

2. Who wrote *The Call of the Wild*, in which a huge pet dog has alarming adventures?

3. By inoculation against what illness did Louis Pasteur save the life of nine-year-old Joseph Meister?

4. Who was the British hero on the Plains of Abraham?

5. What was discovered in France by schoolboys, after their dog fell into a hole?

6. Who is the heroic opponent of the villainous Carl Peterson?

7. In which country were dogs first trained to guide the blind?

8. Who attempted to depict movement in his futurist painting *Dynamism of a Dog on a Leash*?

9. Which Irish nationalist sailed from France in 1798 to invade Ireland, with a force of 14,000 French soldiers?

10. Which Dutch scientist with a powerful new microscope was the first to observe spermatozoa, in the semen of a dog?

31

1. In which British city did the event take place that became known as the Peterloo Massacre?

2. Which two British political parties merged to form the Liberal Democrats?

3. Which artist immortalized some of those who were using London's Underground stations as air-raid shelters?

4. What made Lindow Moss, in Cheshire, famous in 1984?

5. Who wrote the trilogy of plays beginning with *Chicken Soup with Barley*?

6. What name was given to the dense and rapidly rotating form of star first identified by a Cambridge research student and her supervisor?

7. Which thirteen-part television series by David Attenborough told in vivid detail the story of evolution?

8. Whose body was hanged, drawn and quartered at Tyburn in 1661?

9. Which was the first stone bridge built anywhere in a tidal waterway?

10. Which march, written by a Royal Marine bandleader in 1913, was made even more famous by a David Lean film?

32

1. What was the subject of the official deception revealed by *The New York Times* in the Pentagon Papers?

2. Which pretender to the throne occupied by Henry VII was thought so harmless that he was employed in the royal kitchens?

3. What supposedly false name does Jack Worthing use when he is in town?

4. Who was the supposed medieval author of the poem *Fingal*, discovered in 1762?

5. In what sense was the public deceived in 1847 by Currer and Ellis Bell?

6. Who did the three False Dmitrys claim to be the son of?

7. For the supposed discovery of what is Charles Dawson notorious?

8. Which young poet's suicide in a London garret was powerfully depicted in a pre-Raphaelite painting by Henry Wallis?

9. Which forged letter helped give the Conservatives a massive victory in a British general election in the 1920s?

10. Which confidence man confessed with the help of Thomas Mann?

33

1. Which famous song was written by Jack Norworth and Nora Bayes for *The Follies of 1908*?

2. Who succeeded Kofi Annan as the UN Secretary-General?

3. The astronauts in which spacecraft were the first to see the earth rising above the moon's horizon?

4. Who launched the Unification Church as a mission to unify world Christianity?

5. The *Apollo* 15 astronauts David Scott and James Irwin were the first to do what on the moon?

6. Which planet's largest moon, Titan, was first observed by the Dutch astronomer Christiaan Huygens?

7. As music for which film did Richard Addinsell write the *Warsaw Concerto*?

8. Which moons did Galileo observe after he developed a powerful new telescope?

9. Which Mexican poet's first collection was entitled *Wild Moon*?

10. Which French film pioneer used trick effects for his film *Journey to the Moon*?

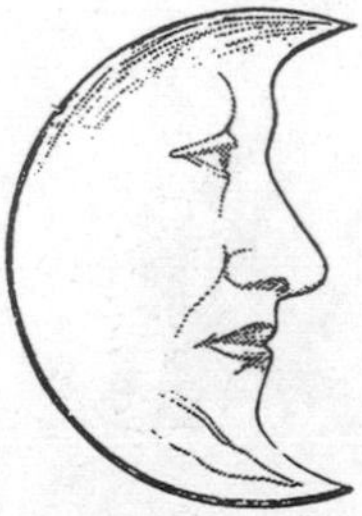

34

1. Which eponymous hero's conception is described in some detail in the first scene of an eighteenth-century novel?

2. Who is the suburban anti-hero of *The Diary of a Nobody*?

3. Which hero commanded the American ship *Bonhomme Richard* in a clash with the British *Serapis* off Flamborough Head?

4. Who introduced a new heroic tradition in US landscape painting with his *Kaaterskill Falls*?

5. Of which country is Skanderbeg the national hero?

6. Who has become known as the 'father of history', owing to his account of the Greco-Persian Wars?

7. For the funeral of which musical hero did vast crowds line the streets of Milan at the start of the twentieth century?

8. Which poem by Alexander Pope introduced a delicate vein of mock-heroism into English literature?

9. Which Greek hero devised various forms of steam engine?

10. Which ever-youthful hero owns a hidden portrait that grows old and ugly?

35

1. Which city did the Babenberg dynasty adopt as their capital in the twelfth century?

2. Which river was chosen as the one on which the capital city of the newly independent USA would be sited?

3. Timur, or Tamburlaine, brought massive quantities of loot from Delhi to his capital city in central Asia – which city?

4. Which Peruvian people's capital city was San Lorenzo until replaced by La Venta?

5. On which river did Alexander the Great's general Seleucus found a new capital city, calling it Seleucia after himself?

6. Which city in Japan became the new imperial capital in the late eighth century?

7. Which impressive new capital city was established with access to the Baltic in the early eighteenth century?

8. Which ancient city became the capital of a new nation in 1871?

9. Which people selected a site for their capital, Tenochtitlan, that has developed into Mexico City?

10. On which African river did the Fatimids establish a new capital city in the tenth century, calling it Al Kahira ('the victorious')?

36

1. What first rolled off the production line at the Piquette Avenue Plant in Detroit in 1908?

2. Who was pardoned for any past misdeeds by Gerald Ford, early in his term of office?

3. The first two towns captured by the Normans in Ireland both begin with 'W' – which were they?

4. Who transformed Abbotsford into a romantic house that he called his 'conundrum castle'?

5. In the gaol of which town did John Bunyan spend eleven years for unlicensed preaching?

6. Which radio company began Britain's first regular broadcasts, from its 2MT station near Chelmsford?

7. Douglas Fairbanks, Charlie Chaplin and D. W. Griffith were three of the four founders of United Artists. Who was the fourth?

8. Which early industrial entrepreneur pioneered the factory environment with his cotton mill at Cromford, Derbyshire?

9. What was the original name of the Bullnose Morris?

10. Which famous story was first told by a lecturer in mathematics to a ten-year-old girl on a boating trip in Oxford?

37

1. What was the previous name of New York?

2. Who wrote the earliest texts in the New Testament?

3. What is the modern name for the new human retrovirus discovered by Luc Montagnier at the Pasteur Institute, called by him LAV?

4. Who launched a new craze for Highland dress when he visited Edinburgh in a tartan kilt?

5. The boat that broke the water speed record in the 1890s derived its name from its newly invented steam turbine. What was the name?

6. Who established Britain's first primary school, at New Lanark in Scotland?

7. Abd-ar-Rahman, escaping from a massacre of his family in Syria, established a new Umayyad dynasty in which country?

8. Who became General Manager of the newly formed British Broadcasting Company?

9. Which outlaw was shot in the back in 1882 by a new member of his gang, working secretly for the police?

10. Which new opposition party confronted the Sadducees in the second century BC?

38

1. *Prester John*, published in the early twentieth century, was the first adventure story by which British writer?

2. Who gave the world's first demonstration of television, to a group assembled in his attic rooms in London?

3. Which English poet was *Summoned by Bells* in the title of a long autobiographical poem?

4. Which two authors, separated by a generation, met first in the London bookshop of Thomas Davies?

5. Which composer wrote an opera featuring a US president on a visit abroad?

6. Who was buried darkly at dead of night, with the sods turned by bayonet?

7. Which religious reformer was put in charge of the Bethlehem Chapel in Prague in the early fifteenth century?

8. Which admiral was shot on the deck of a ship in Portsmouth Harbour?

9. Which British army officer was executed in New York as a spy?

10. Which basketball champion began a twelve-year career with the Los Angeles Lakers in the 1980s?

39

1. To which area of Canada did the greatest number of Loyalists migrate, fleeing British America in the 1780s?

2. Who led a revolt by fellow slaves in Southampton County, Virginia, in the 1830s?

3. Who claimed to have made landfall at three places in North America, naming one of them Vinland?

4. Which tribal group was driven west to the Great Lakes by Iroquois raids in the mid seventeenth century?

5. Who led the Nation of Islam, or Black Muslims, for more than forty years from 1934?

6. Which of the fifty states of the United States is not in North America?

7. Which phrase from Ecclesiasticus was used by James Agee and Walker Evans as the title for their warm personal view of America?

8. Who traced his family origins back to Africa in his book *Roots*?

9. In which river valley are there burial mounds, built first in the Adena culture and then by Hopewell tribes?

10. Whose title to what was recognized by the Supreme Court of Canada in the Calder case?

40

1. The horrors of what natural phenomenon in Oklahoma forced John Steinbeck's Joad family to travel west?

2. In which country had the horrors happened that became the subject of Roland Joffé's 1984 film *The Killing Fields*?

3. In which novel does space-traveller Billy Pilgrim suffer horrors?

4. Which British prime minister wrote an influential pamphlet with the title *Bulgarian Horrors*?

5. Which English novelist was credited with creating what he called the 'super-horror' storyline of *King Kong*?

6. Which musical by Howard Ashman and Alan Menken opened off-Broadway in 1982?

7. Which novel of 1886 was the basis of the first horror film, made by the Polyscope Film Company in 1908?

8. Which movie, directed by William Friedkin, was adapted from a novel by William Peter Blatty?

9. Who painted *Gassed*, a powerful image of one of the particular horrors of the First World War?

10. What was the title of the first of Stephen King's many horror novels?

41

1. Where had the prisoners been captured who were released by Fidel Castro in return for $53 million in food and medicine?

2. Who wrote *Pisan Cantos*, about his post-war imprisonment in an American detention centre near Pisa?

3. What did Thomas Malory write while in prison somewhere in England?

4. Who was jailed for thirty days for opening the first US birth control clinic?

5. Which German leader negotiated in the 1950s the release of the last 10,000 German prisoners of war held in the USSR?

6. Who claimed, in the title of her first novel, to know why the caged bird sings?

7. From which German ship, in use as a floating prison, were 303 merchant seamen rescued in a daring British raid during the Second World War?

8. Which prison reformer was shocked into action by the conditions he saw in Bedford Gaol?

9. Which French king was taken prisoner by the Spanish at the Battle of Pavia?

10. Which emperor was held prisoner in his final years by his son, in Agra's Red Fort?

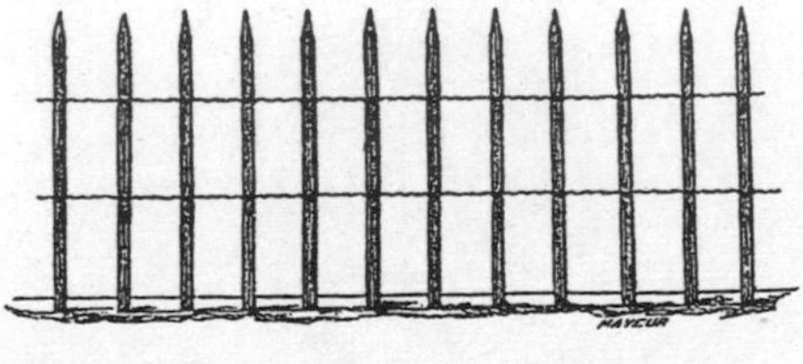

42

1. In which modern African country did the Marinids bring an end to the rule of the Almohads in the thirteenth century?

2. Which British author and politician galloped into battle at Omdurman with the 21st Lancers?

3. Which New York dance company toured South Africa with the slogan 'Dancing Through Barriers'?

4. Who led a disastrous raid into the Transvaal, in an attempt to expel Paul Kruger?

5. Which guerrilla group fought from the 1960s for Mozambique's independence?

6. Which military caste ruled Egypt from the thirteenth century, replacing Saladin's dynasty?

7. Which group of people won a victory at Vegkop in 1837, after which they massacred the neighbouring villagers?

8. Where are hieroglyphic Egyptian, demotic Egyptian and Greek found together in the same very durable document?

9. In the line of succession at the time, what was unusual about Hatshepsut?

10. Tribes of which linguistic group formed the powerful Maravi Confederacy in the region of Lake Nysasa in the late fifteenth century?

43

1. To frustrate which group of people was Britain's Cat and Mouse Act of 1913 devised?

2. For which painting did Holman Hunt travel all the way to the Dead Sea to achieve an authentic landscape?

3. For what purpose did landlords remove crofters from their estates in Scotland's Highland Clearances?

4. What was the real name of Buffalo Bill?

5. What astronomical feature derives its name from the Greek for 'circle of animals'?

6. What name is given to the battle in which Ali defeated Aisha, one of the wives of Muhammad?

7. Which mutiny, leading to a war of independence, was provoked by the use of animal fat?

8. What did an Arab goatherd find in a cave in the Qumran desert in the 1940s?

9. In which Chinese dynasty did brightly coloured camels take their place among the tomb attendants?

10. Which pioneering photographer published *Animal Locomotion*, using successive still images to display the process of motion?

44

1. What name became used for medieval England's department of finance, derived from a table on which instant calculations could be made?

2. Why did the first Greek translation of the Old Testament become known as the Septuagint?

3. By what name has Tsar Ivan IV become known?

4. Which great Bohemian leader developed a form of mobile barricade that became known as his 'war wagon fortress'?

5. By what name did *Quotations from Chairman Mao Zedong* become better known?

6. What name was given to the 1810 uprising against Spanish rule in Mexico launched by a parish priest in Dolores?

7. By what name are the first ten amendments to the US Constitution collectively known?

8. What did the mass political demonstrations organized in Ireland by Daniel O'Connell become known as?

9. What constellation of seven stars was used as the name for seven French poets in a group that included Ronsard?

10. In which country did a reforming party become known as the Liberales, in the first political use of the term 'Liberal'?

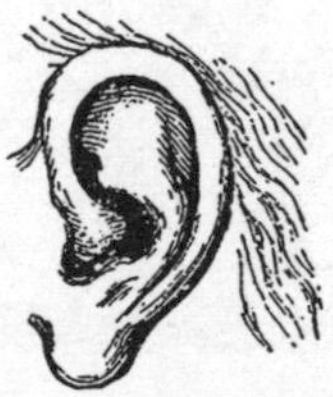

45

1. Of what did the two-year-old Puyi become the last example?

2. What phrase was used during the Chinese Cultural Revolution to denounce Communist leaders Liu Shaoqi and Deng Xiaoping as friends of capitalism?

3. Chopsticks survive in China from more than 3000 years ago. What are they made of?

4. At the north end of which square is China's Gate of Heavenly Peace?

5. Which emperor called his new dynasty Ta Yuan (Great Origin)?

6. What, until recently, was the name by which the west knew Jiang Jieshi, who set up a national Chinese government in the 1920s?

7. What event linked Jiangxi province to Shaanxi in 1934–5?

8. What name is given to the popular rising at the start of the twentieth century against foreign intrusion into China?

9. Who was sent out by George III as the first British ambassador to the Chinese empire?

10. Which is the first great Chinese dynasty, dating from about 1600 BC?

46

1. What semi-secret organization was formed by three British art students in the 1840s?

2. Whose harmony class did Pierre Boulez join at the Paris Conservatoire?

3. What radical change in admissions policy was first introduced in the USA by Oberlin College in Ohio?

4. Whose elder brother Alexander was executed, while still a student, for his part in a plot to execute the tsar, Alexander III?

5. What name did Mullah Mohammed Omar give to the group of fundamentalist students he formed in Kandahar?

6. Whose beauty caused havoc among the male students of Oxford in a novel of the early twentieth century?

7. At which university in Ohio were four students killed by National Guards during an anti-Vietnam War demonstration?

8. Which two students at Columbia University began a very successful working partnership with their musical *Fly With Me*?

9. Which Jesuit missionary became the first Western student of Chinese civilization?

10. Which eighteen-year-old student in Apollonia was given the news that he had been named successor to Julius Caesar?

47

1. What creatures were proved by Karl von Frisch to calculate direction by the polarized light of the sun?

2. What was the title of Ernest Hemingway's second novel, which is also known as *Fiesta*?

3. What was the title of Alan Sillitoe's first novel?

4. Which film of 1960 was directed by Jules Dassin and starred Melina Mercouri?

5. For which Memphis company did a US truck driver make his first commercial recordings?

6. Which fourteen-year-old danced the sun god Apollo in a court ballet and found that he rather liked the role?

7. By what name did a statue in Rhodes of Helios, the Greek sun god, become widely known?

8. Of which galaxy is our sun a part?

9. What term of abuse for a style of art was inspired by Claude Monet's painting of a sunrise?

10. What name did William Lever give to the model village he built for workers in his factory?

48

1. What was the simple name of London's first theatre, built by James Burbage?

2. What kind of theatre was launched by Eugène Ionesco's play *The Bald Prima Donna*?

3. In what kind of theatre did Joseph Lister make a life-saving innovation?

4. Which Russian prime minister was assassinated on a visit to a theatre in Kiev?

5. What great theatrical tradition began when Kanami and Zeami Motokiyo pleased a shogun in the fourteenth century?

6. Which is the earliest and best surviving example of the classical Greek stage and auditorium?

7. Which designer, the son of Ellen Terry, published a manifesto under the title *The Art of the Theatre*?

8. Which famous movie-theatre organ was first put on the market in 1911?

9. Who assassinated President Lincoln in his box at the theatre?

10. Which six-year-old gave his first professional performance in a pier theatre in New Jersey, with his sister Adele?

49

1. Who designed the tomb for Oscar Wilde in the Père Lachaise cemetery in Paris?

2. Which emperor is buried in an austerely impressive tomb at Pasagardae?

3. Many of the paintings of Piero della Francesca are still to be seen in his home town. What is its name?

4. In which city does the Mughal emperor Humayn have a magnificent domed tomb?

5. In which modern country is Djenné, famous for the terracotta figures found in medieval graves?

6. Which pope commissioned Michelangelo to design an elaborate tomb for him?

7. Where is Britain's Tomb of the Unknown Warrior?

8. The tombs excavated at Vergina, in Macedonia, are thought to include that of which king?

9. Where in Egypt is the famous 'step pyramid', which was built as the tomb of the pharaoh Djoser?

10. What type of tomb is the so-called Treasury of Atreus, at Mycenae?

50

1. What name was given to the fabulously wealthy Christian king somewhere in the east, of whom news began to filter west in the twelfth century?

2. Who founded a newspaper, *Il Popolo d'Italia* (*The People of Italy*), to argue the case for Italy to join the First World War on the side of the Allies?

3. What controversial step by the Danish newspaper *Jyllands-Posten* (*The Jutland Post*) provoked violent protests in many parts of the world?

4. Which London weekly journal was the first to offer its readers the enticement of colour illustrations?

5. The first news of the victory at Waterloo was given to the British government by a private citizen – who?

6. Which English journalist launched a weekly newspaper, *The Political Register*, which he continued till his death in 1835?

7. In which country were news sheets first published, in the early seventeenth century?

8. Which British consul (executed by the British thirteen years later) revealed news of appalling abuses by Belgian companies in the Congo Free State?

9. What was the name of the act of parliament by which Britain imposed a tax on newspapers in the American colonies?

10. What significant breakthrough in the production of newspapers was achieved by *The Times* near the end of the Napoleonic Wars?

51

1. Which early civilization produced delicate seals in a script that is as yet undeciphered?

2. Who called his new discovery x-rays, because their nature was as yet unknown?

3. Which British scholar deciphered Linear B, the script of Mycenae?

4. Which US astronomer predicted the existence of an unknown planet, almost exactly where Pluto was discovered twenty-five years later?

5. Where is America's Tomb of the Unknowns?

6. Which German foreign minister sent a telegram which caused outrage when it was deciphered in the USA, because it promised to give Texas to Mexico?

7. What geographical term is derived from the Latin phrase for an 'unknown southern land'?

8. Which painter, almost unknown at the time, spent several months in a psychiatric asylum at St Rémy towards the end of his life?

9. Which work was commissioned by an unknown stranger who arrived mysteriously in Vienna in the early 1790s?

10. Which previously unknown American blues singer was first recorded singing in the Louisiana State Penitentiary?

52

1. Which previous winner did Sophocles defeat when he won the prize for tragedy in Athens in 468 BC?

2. Whose party won a landslide victory in the Burmese election of 1946?

3. Which partnership was defeated by Octavian in a sea battle in 31 BC?

4. Who wrote 'Heart of Oak' to celebrate a British naval victory over the French in 1759?

5. Which Belgian cyclist retired after a fourteen-year career with a record 445 victories?

6. Who were the victors when Mikhail Gorbachev announced that Soviet troops would leave Afghanistan?

7. In what context did *Bluenose* bring a series of international victories for Canada?

8. Who suffered a massive defeat in the 1991 presidential election in Zambia?

9. Who led the Likud party to victory in the election of 1996?

10. Who commanded the victorious army at the Battle of the Pyramids?

53

1. In which religion was there a doctrinal split as to whether one should go 'sky clad' (naked) or 'white clad' (wearing a simple robe)?

2. Which White Star liner made her maiden voyage from Southampton in 1912?

3. In which London street was Charles I beheaded?

4. Which US president was the first to move into the White House?

5. In what sport was Jess Willard the 'Great White Hope'?

6. Which group of people achieved a heroic Ice March in 1918, but to no good end?

7. How did William the Aetheling, heir to the English throne, die?

8. Which battle ended the brief reign of Frederick V in Bohemia?

9. What was commanded by the English *condottiere* John Hawkwood in fourteenth-century Italy?

10. Of whom did John White produce famous images in the 1580s?

54

1. In which film did the twelve-year-old Elizabeth Taylor have a horse as her co-star?

2. What did horses enable Otto van Guericke to demonstrate the power of in the mid seventeenth century?

3. Who was leader of the group that brought the first horses to America?

4. In the same year as *The Sheik* was released, Rudolph Valentino starred in another famous film – which?

5. What is the name of the annual horse race in Siena?

6. On what occasion was there an encounter between Emily Davison and a racehorse?

7. Which Liverpool artist became England's best-known painter of horses?

8. What French word, meaning 'hobby horse', was selected at random as the name for a new artistic movement in 1916?

9. In which London stadium did the first International Horse Show take place?

10. Which Turk forms a trio with the Darley Arabian and the Godolphin Arabian?

55

1. Who killed his royal cousin in a battle near Elgin in the eleventh century?

2. Which composer founded the St Magnus Festival in the Orkneys?

3. In what sense did the lack of 'w' in the French alphabet affect the Scottish royal house?

4. Which medieval Scottish philosopher unwittingly provided the English language with the word 'dunce'?

5. In which village did government soldiers, mainly Campbells, massacre their MacDonald hosts?

6. Which lover of Mary, Queen of Scots, almost certainly instigated the murder of her husband?

7. What event brought to an abrupt end the hopes of Charles Edward Stuart?

8. What was new about the *Charlotte Dundas* when it went into service in 1802?

9. Which political group derived their name from an agreement signed in an Edinburgh churchyard in the 1630s?

10. What was banned by the British government in 1746, in a restriction not lifted until 1782?

56

1. Which early English novelist wrote a fictional life of Jonathan Wild, billed as a great thief-taker?

2. Whom did Queen Victoria describe as 'an old, wild and incomprehensible man of eighty-two and a half'?

3. In which civilization were elephants first tamed and put to work?

4. Who directed Marilyn Monroe, Tony Curtis and Jack Lemmon in *Some Like It Hot*?

5. In which part of the world were horses first tamed, bred from and eventually ridden?

6. Which US novelist and dramatist wrote the play *Our Town*?

7. Oscar Wilde was one of the two most prominent members of the Aesthetic Movement in Britain. Who was the other?

8. Which US children's author and illustrator wrote the classic *Where the Wild Things Are*?

9. What word, meaning 'wild beasts', was used by a critic to ridicule the work of Matisse, Derain and others?

10. What name did William Cody give to his entertainment depicting the world of the cowboy?

57

1. In which US city did an act of home-grown terrorism destroy federal buildings and 168 people?

2. What sect was inspired by Ann Lee, who crossed the Atlantic to America in 1774 to spread the word?

3. What was the purpose of the Black Codes, introduced by the defeated Southern states in the 1860s?

4. What became the most famous of Charles Fourier's utopian communities in the USA, established at Dedham, near Boston?

5. In response to American protests, the British government removed the Townshend duties on all commodities except one. Which was the exception?

6. What name did Robert de la Salle give to the entire Mississippi region, in honour of his king?

7. The US public was outraged to discover in 1798 that the French were asking for bribes – by what three letters is this 'affair' known?

8. With what kind of disaster is New York's Triangle Shirtwaist Company associated?

9. Which influential US architectural critic wrote *The Culture of Cities*?

10. Whose death was lamented by Walt Whitman in his Civil War poem 'O Captain! My Captain!'?

58

1. Who composed a song cycle about a beautiful miller's wife?

2. Who wrote *The Misfits* for his wife?

3. Which novel begins with a future mayor selling his wife at a fair?

4. Whose wife was largely responsible for the Beijing ballet *The Red Detachment of Women*?

5. Which famous building is a memorial to a much-lamented wife, whose name meant 'pearl of the palace'?

6. Who established a theatre company with his wife, Madeleine Renaud, at the Théâtre Marigny in Paris?

7. What did Nebuchadnezzar build supposedly to comfort a homesick wife?

8. Who painted a very stark image of his wife and himself naked, entitled *The Leg of Mutton Nude*?

9. In which castle did Edward II die, almost certainly murdered on the orders of his wife and her lover?

10. Who was the first husband of the wife of John Everett Millais?

59

1. Which bridge in Rome, still standing, was built for the Roman emperor Hadrian?

2. Which play by Arthur Miller tells the story of Eddie Carbone, an Italian-American longshoreman?

3. Of what type were the two bridges that Thomas Telford completed in the same year at Conwy and the Menai Strait?

4. Which of Sydney's two defining landmarks was completed in 1932?

5. In which battle in 1297 did William Wallace inflict a severe defeat on an English army?

6. On what great project by Isambard Kingdom Brunel did construction work begin in 1836?

7. Which 1957 film, directed by David Lean, had William Holden and Jack Hawkins as two of its three leading actors?

8. What major climatic change enabled human beings to migrate from Siberia to Alaska about 30,000 years ago?

9. Before what battle did the Roman emperor Constantine order his men to wear a Christian symbol, the Chi-Rho, on their shields?

10. The Verrazano-Narrows Bridge links Brooklyn with which island?

60

1. In which country was paper money first used?

2. Which German banking family had a valuable relationship with the Habsburg Dynasty, after first lending money to an archduke in 1487?

3. Which giant Texas company filed for bankruptcy early in the twenty-first century, after the disclosure of major accountancy fraud?

4. Which city was granted valuable trading privileges by Constantinople in the eleventh century, with exemption from all dues and customs?

5. Which prosperous ancient trading city, in modern Jordan, is famous for its classical tombs carved in the rock?

6. Which great company, registered in New Jersey, was broken up by US anti-trust legislation early in the twentieth century?

7. What was the name given by Mao Zedong to the disastrous economic policy that he introduced in 1958?

8. Which country's national bank, founded in the mid seventeenth century, is still in business today as the world's oldest bank?

9. Samuel de Champlain founded Quebec as a centre for what trade?

10. People of what kind were protected by the Joint Stock Companies Act passed in the early nineteenth century in Britain?

61

1. Who designed an early iron and glass conservatory for the Duke of Devonshire at Chatsworth?

2. Who was in Jerusalem at the start of a rebellion against the Romans, which he later described in his *Jewish War*?

3. Which future novelist went to sea with the British Merchant Navy in 1878?

4. What title did Boston merchant Samuel Sewall give to his pamphlet protesting against the slave trade?

5. Which German artist achieved prominence when he walked round a gallery demonstrating *How to Explain Pictures to a Dead Hare*?

6. In what did Scottish chemist Joseph Black observe the phenomenon of latent heat?

7. By what name is Joseph Ratzinger now better known?

8. Who was the best known of the botanists on Captain Cook's first expedition to the Pacific?

9. Which English chemist isolated oxygen but believed it to be 'dephlogisticated air'?

10. Which King Joseph was abruptly transferred from the throne of Naples to that of Spain in the early nineteenth century?

62

1. What simple and literal name was given to the town and abbey founded to celebrate the great Portuguese victory at Aljubarrota?

2. Which battle ended with the surrender to the Vietminh of 12,000 French troops?

3. Who was at last secure in his kingdom after his victory at Bannockburn?

4. Which British general halted the advance of Rommel, in the first battle of El Alamein?

5. Which very successful rebel was defeated and killed by the future Edward I at Evesham?

6. Which ridge was taken in the First World War by Canadian troops and is now the site of Canada's most important war memorial?

7. Which Celtic leader defeated Julius Caesar at Gergovia in 52 BC but was captured later in the year?

8. In which graveyard was the battle fought that brought to an end the brief rule of the Paris Communards?

9. Where did James II and William III confront each other on a battlefield?

10. In what sense was the Battle of Lepanto the last of its kind?

63

1. Which artist, with a studio in Wittenberg, had a profitable line in naked female figures from mythology?

2. Which iconic figure is less well known as Lisa Gherardini?

3. For what type of painting is the Dutch artist Aelbert Cuyp best known?

4. What name is used for the rooms in the Vatican that have frescoes by Raphael?

5. Painters of what kind of object developed the black-figure style in the sixth century BC?

6. What name is given to the style of painting in dots that was developed in particular by Seurat?

7. Which group of people are portrayed in the realistic wax portraits found in coffins at Fayyum?

8. What name is given to the late medieval style of European painting noted for its slender and elegant figures?

9. For what type of painting in particular did the New York artist Jean-Michel Basquiat become famous?

10. Which French artist caused a sensation with his painting *Nude Descending a Staircase, No. 2*?

64

1. Which cousin and rival did Stephen take care to keep off the English throne?

2. The Pylon group of British poets in the 1930s derived their name from the title of a poem by which of their members?

3. Which film involving a terrified motorist launched Steven Spielberg's career as a movie director?

4. Which snooker player won the first of six world championship titles in the early 1980s?

5. Who came to national prominence through his debates with Stephen Douglas, his rival for an Illinois seat in the US Senate?

6. Which film by Stephen Daldry follows an English boy's journey from a mining community to the world of dance?

7. Which marching song of the Union forces was used by Stephen V. Benét as the title of his verse narrative of the American Civil War?

8. In which state of the USA was American settlement begun by Stephen Austin?

9. Which founder of Black Consciousness died of head wounds in police custody?

10. Which very successful computer product was launched by a pair of Steves in the 1970s?

65

1. Of what was Glenn Curtis's *Flying Fish* the first example?

2. Which much-improved sailing vessel, developed in the Mediterranean, was adapted by the Portuguese for Atlantic use?

3. In which town on the Thames was the first Oxford and Cambridge Boat Race held?

4. Which Spanish composer died when the Channel steamer *Sussex* was torpedoed by a U-boat?

5. In what way did a barge pulled by a horse look unusual at Pont Cysyllte after 1805?

6. Where was an Anglo-Saxon king buried in a ship with his treasure?

7. In what film did Paul Robeson sing 'Ol' Man River'?

8. What was the name of the balsa wood boat constructed by Thor Heyerdahl?

9. What was new about the *Clermont*, launched on the Hudson River by US engineer Robert Fulton?

10. What is the title of the poem which features a 'dirty British coaster'?

66

1. What was recently demoted to the status of a 'dwarf planet'?

2. Who was the first woman in space?

3. What name did William Herschel give to the planet he discovered in 1781, now known as Uranus?

4. Which Swedish astronomer proposed a gap of 100 degrees between the freezing and boiling points of water?

5. What caused a widely publicized handshake between Tom Stafford and Aleksei Leonov?

6. Which new calendar was introduced in the papal states in 1582?

7. Gaspra and Ida were in the news in the early 1990s. Who or what are they?

8. Which medieval mathematician and astronomer also wrote romantic four-line verses in his spare time?

9. What prediction by Edmond Halley came precisely true sixteen years after his death?

10. What was the name of the first living creature to visit space from earth?

67

1. Which artist published four great volumes entitled *Birds of America*?

2. Whose first novel was *A Summer Birdcage*?

3. What name was given to the new grappling device which helped the Roman fleet to defeat the Carthaginians at Mylae in 260 BC?

4. Who was the original choreographer of Stravinsky's ballet *The Firebird*?

5. What method of sending messages home was pioneered by the rulers of Baghdad in the eleventh century?

6. Who was known by the nickname Yardbird, or simply Bird?

7. Martha, who died in Cincinnati Zoo, was the last of her kind – what kind?

8. Which US author published her first, only and immensely successful novel in 1960?

9. Which novel has brought Sebastian Faulks his greatest success?

10. Which composer combined birdsong with piano and orchestra in his *Waking of the Birds*?

68

1. Whose two books published in the same year, *Émile* and *Du Contrat Social*, prompted orders for his arrest?

2. Which two orders were the first to be established for the capitals of Greek pillars?

3. Who divided his possessions to form two Habsburg empires, the Austrian and the Spanish?

4. Whose last film was *Two-Faced Woman*, which received terrible reviews, partly prompting her retirement?

5. Into which two major groups did the Goths split?

6. Which pair made their first appearance in *The Man with Two Left Feet*?

7. Who was reported to have taken only two days to run from Athens to Sparta to ask for help against the Persians?

8. Which are the 'two cities' in the title of Charles Dickens's novel?

9. Who spent two self-sufficient years in a hut at Walden Pond and then published an account of it?

10. Two of Jane Austen's novels were published in the year after her death. *Northanger Abbey* was one. What was the other?

69

1. What property in Scotland did Victoria and Albert purchase in 1852?

2. What in particular has made the castle church in Wittenberg famous?

3. With whom did George Canning fight a duel in which he was wounded?

4. Who ceded his crown to a rival and a few months later died in Pontefract Castle, probably starved to death?

5. Outside which papal castle did the emperor Henry IV stand in penance, to be released from excommunication?

6. Which US poet's second collection had the title *Lord Weary's Castle*?

7. In which castle is the Scottish National War Memorial?

8. Which palatial fortress was built in the thirteenth century by the Muslim rulers of Granada?

9. Which dynasty took its name from the 'hawk's castle', or Habichtsburg, which they built near Zurich in the eleventh century?

10. What was the title of Edmund Wilson's collection of essays about symbolist writers?

70

1. Which two photographers set up the Little Galleries of the Photo-Secession in New York?

2. For what public-spirited purpose did John D. Rockefeller, Jr, donate land along New York's East River in the 1940s?

3. Who reached and explored, in the early seventeenth century, the river that flows past the west side of Manhattan?

4. Which fictional Dutch scholar supposedly wrote the comic *History of New York*, published in the early nineteenth century?

5. How did Elisha Otis dramatically demonstrate his new device to make elevators safe, in New York's Crystal Palace in 1854?

6. In which novel did Tom Wolfe give a bleak view of contemporary New York?

7. The *New York World* included in 1913 the first example of something that became a worldwide passion – what?

8. To which state did the Brooklyn Dodgers and the New York Giants move, in the same year?

9. What title did Damon Runyon use for his first collection of stories about low life in New York?

10. What is the more familiar name for the International Exhibition of Modern Art, which was a sensation in New York just before the First World War?

71

1. At which city did the Turks lob vast stones from a nineteen-ton gun of cast iron in 1453?

2. By what last-ditch tactic did the Dutch save the town of Alkmaar from falling into the hands of the Spanish?

3. Whose company produced the Pup and the Camel in the First World War?

4. Who provided the armour and weapons for soldiers in ancient Greece's 'citizen armies'?

5. Which nation was the first to get a jet aircraft into aerial combat?

6. How many wars did Britain fight and lose against Afghanistan between 1838 and 1921?

7. In which battle did US planes sink four Japanese aircraft carriers, halting for the first time Japan's aggressive expansion?

8. Against which enemy did American warships win a victory on Lake Erie in 1813?

9. What was the agreed dividing line between north and south at the end of the Korean War?

10. What change was made to the border between the two countries at the end of the Iran–Iraq War, with more than a million dead?

72

1. In what sense was *Don Juan*, starring John Barrymore, a first in 1926?

2. To which poet does *Il Postino* deliver mail?

3. Which film by Sergei Eisenstein was set during the Russian Revolution of 1905?

4. Which film of the early 1990s had Jodie Foster and Anthony Hopkins as co-stars?

5. Which director had a great success with his first film, *Pather Panchali*?

6. Which nostalgic film of the late 1990s triggered a cult for Cuban music?

7. In which film, directed by Zhang Zimou, does Gong Li play one of the concubines of a Chinese warlord?

8. In which film did Woody Allen make his screen debut?

9. Which of Laurence Olivier's films, released during the Second World War, had stirring music by William Walton?

10. Which musical film starred the seventeen-year-old Judy Garland in 1939?

73

1. What was the name of the black panther that taught Mowgli about the jungle?

2. Who directed *Crouching Tiger, Hidden Dragon*?

3. What shortened name is commonly used for the LTTE, a violent separatist movement in Sri Lanka?

4. Who commissioned a magnificent relief of a lion hunt for his new palace at Nineveh?

5. What lasting name was acquired by a British rugby team touring South Africa in the 1920s?

6. Which Scottish king was captured raiding into Northumberland and was taken south with his feet tied beneath his horse?

7. Of which culture was the Tomb of the Lionesses, in Tarquinia, a part?

8. Which two of the four major championships did Tiger Woods win in his first year as a golf professional?

9. In which culture were cats treated as sacred animals in temples?

10. What was the title of the book in which C. S. Lewis introduced Narnia to his readers?

74

1. Which Shakespeare play was being performed when the Globe Theatre caught fire?

2. Who persuaded the people of Florence to throw playing cards and lewd images on a great 'bonfire of vanities'?

3. Who set up a Tire and Rubber Company in Akron, Ohio, at the start of the twentieth century?

4. In which novel does Vladimir Nabokov tell his story through an editor's annotations to a poem?

5. Who was the Roman goddess of the hearth, in whose shrine virgin priestesses tended a sacred flame?

6. Which plane, designed by Reginald Mitchell, had its first test flight three years before the Second World War?

7. Which 1981 film dramatized the rivalry between two British athletes at the 1924 Olympics?

8. With which patriotic and topical song did Ivor Novello have a great success at the start of the First World War?

9. What name did President Roosevelt give to his informal radio broadcasts to the US people?

10. Which US city was largely destroyed by fire in 1906, after an exceptionally violent earthquake?

75

1. Where was the prison to which Nelson Mandela was sent after being sentenced to life imprisonment?

2. Who wrote the Latin text *The Consolation of Philosophy* while in prison in Pavia?

3. What is the meaning of the title of John Cage's 1952 composition *4′33″*?

4. Who was in prison in Genoa when he was persuaded by a fellow prisoner to write down his remarkable adventures?

5. Outside which prison did London's last public executions take place?

6. Who conducted fellow prisoners in Holloway in a suffragette anthem composed by herself?

7. In what environment was the US poet Philip Freneau held by the British for six weeks, resulting in an influential poem?

8. Which Quaker philanthropist campaigned on behalf of female prisoners after seeing the conditions in London's Newgate Gaol?

9. Which German theologian, in Buchenwald, wrote *Letters and Papers from Prison*?

10. Which English revolutionary spent nearly a year in a French prison after opposing the execution of Louis XVI?

76

1. Which British explorer sailed round Tasmania, discovering the strait that now bears his name?

2. A young American architect, Walter B. Griffin, won a competition in 1913 to design what?

3. What was returned to the Aboriginal Mutijulu people and given its original name, Uluru?

4. What was launched in 1923 as Australia's answer to Marmite?

5. What was the name of the controversial policy attacked in the pamphlet *Control or Colour Bar?*

6. In which book did Robert Hughes describe the penal system of colonial Australia?

7. What was Australia's first mass-produced car, which rolled off the production line in 1948?

8. In honour of which Australian singer did Auguste Escoffier create and name a dessert?

9. Which prime minister went for a swim in heavy surf and was never seen again?

10. As what did Albert Namatjira achieve success and fame?

77

1. To the court of which Mughal emperor was Sir Thomas Roe sent as Britain's first ambassador to India?

2. Whom did the US House Judiciary Committee accuse in 1974 of obstruction of justice?

3. On what subject did the US Supreme Court make a highly inflammatory judgment in the Dred Scott case?

4. Who was sent home after being judged mentally incapable to stand trial by the British Home Secretary, Jack Straw?

5. Injustice to whom was Émile Zola protesting about in his famous letter '*J'accuse!*'?

6. Which US sex symbol was sentenced to eight days in prison when her Broadway play *Sex* was judged to be obscene?

7. In what sense was Thurgood Marshall a significant 'first' in the USA?

8. Which US poet published a collection called *The Tennis Court Oath*?

9. Which famous orator made his first appearance in a Roman court in 81 BC?

10. What new economic right was established in Australia by the Harvester Judgment early in the twentieth century?

78

1. Who was the first boxer to become world heavyweight champion three times?

2. Which German engineer built the Tri-Star, a three-wheeled internal-combustion vehicle considered to be the first commercial automobile?

3. Which Australian sprinter won three gold medals in the Melbourne Olympics in 1956?

4. Whose three victories in a single year in the 1740s caused him to be known by his contemporaries as 'the Great'?

5. Which Finnish designer produced a bent-plywood three-legged stool, specifically designed for stacking?

6. Who wrote the music for *The Three-Cornered Hat*, a ballet produced by Diaghilev with choreography by Massine and designs by Picasso?

7. In which country has the ambitious and controversial Three Gorges Dam been completed?

8. Which early play of Shakespeare's consists of three parts?

9. Where, in southern Italy, are there three superb Greek temples dating from the sixth and fifth centuries BC?

10. Who in recent years has won a third term as New Zealand's prime minister?

79

1. What item of clothing distinguished the men parading before Mussolini in Rome after he became prime minister?

2. Who, later famous, worked at the age of twelve in Warren's boot-blacking factory?

3. The roof of which institution features in the final scene of the first British talkie, directed by Alfred Hitchcock?

4. Which publisher commissioned Charles Rennie Mackintosh to build him Hill House, in Helensburgh?

5. From what does 'Hawking radiation' emerge?

6. What was the title of the first collection of essays by W. E. B. Du Bois?

7. A poem about which village craftsman was published by Henry Wadsworth Longfellow in his *Ballads and Other Poems*?

8. What was spread by Turks lobbing infected corpses over the walls of Caffa, where they were besieging Genoese merchants?

9. What nickname was subsequently given to the air and variations in Handel's fifth harpsichord suite in E?

10. What name was later given to the small room in which 122 people died in 1756?

80

1. Who survived alone on a Pacific island for five years, and became the inspiration for *Robinson Crusoe*?

2. What was blown up by French agents in Auckland Harbour?

3. On which island was Captain James Cook killed in a skirmish with natives over a stolen boat?

4. What was first successfully tested at Enewetak Atoll in the Marshall Islands?

5. Which concert, given by Elvis Presley in Honolulu, was the first to be broadcast live round the world?

6. Which volcanic island, south-east of Tokyo, did US troops finally capture in the Second World War at a cost of 20,000 dead?

7. Who was in command of the first ships to cross the Pacific, reaching Guam from South America in ninety-nine days?

8. On which island did US anthropologist Margaret Mead claim to have found a very relaxed attitude to sex among adolescents?

9. Which Pacific islands became a US territory five years after American involvement in the overthrow of the ruling dynasty?

10. Which artist moved to Tahiti in 1891 and spent most of the rest of his life in the Pacific?

81

1. For the host nation, the International Exposition known as Expo 67 was the centrepiece of which particular celebration?

2. What influential organization was founded in Canada in 1971 to campaign against US nuclear testing?

3. Which British peer produced a *Report on the Affairs of British North America* in 1839?

4. What name did Canada's Aboriginal peoples give to the assembly they set up in the 1980s?

5. Which ocean did Alexander Mackenzie reach, exploring by canoe from central Canada?

6. Which author gave his three semi-autobiographical novels the group title *The Deptford Trilogy*?

7. Which Soviet dancer defected from the Kirov company while on tour in Canada in the 1970s?

8. Who developed the concept of the global village in his book *The Gutenberg Galaxy*?

9. Which explorer, searching for a trade route to China, probably reached Newfoundland in the 1490s?

10. What were linked to the sea by the completion of a joint Canadian and US project in the 1950s?

82

1. Which party emerged within the first years of Islam and caused a major schism?

2. What name did Engels persuade a group of radical Germans to adopt, at a congress in London in the 1840s?

3. What shortened name was adopted in 1923 by the South African National Native Congress?

4. Which party, with a pan-Arab political agenda, was founded by Michel Aflaq and others in Syria in the 1940s?

5. What political party was formed in China in the early twentieth century, with Sun Yat-sen as one of its leaders?

6. What new name was adopted soon after the First World War by the small German Workers' Party?

7. Who founded the National Party in South Africa early in the twentieth century?

8. What name became attached to the rival Republican party formed by Theodore Roosevelt in opposition to William Howard Taft?

9. Which group of Italian revolutionaries emerged in early-nineteenth-century Naples in opposition to French rule?

10. What names were used by the first two political parties in the USA, the rival followers of Alexander Hamilton and Thomas Jefferson?

83

1. From which island did the Venetians move their administration to the Rialto in the ninth century?

2. Which island was ceded to Britain at the end of the First Opium War?

3. On an island in which great West African river did the British build Fort James in 1661?

4. To which island was Napoleon sent into exile in 1814?

5. On which island was the Palace of Knossos built?

6. What was the world's leading observatory in the late sixteenth century, built by Danish astronomer Tycho Brahe on the island of Hven?

7. The Spanish, when in sole occupation of the Falkland Islands in the 1770s, gave them a more Spanish name – what name?

8. Which island reverted in the late twentieth century from Portuguese to Chinese ownership?

9. Which country used Devil's Island as a penal colony?

10. On which island of the Outer Hebrides is Compton Mackenzie's *Whisky Galore!* set?

84

1. What book by the Japanese author Murasaki Shikibu, from the early eleventh century, can be considered the world's first novel?

2. Who, according to the Qur'an, are the three 'people of the book'?

3. Which English game is first mentioned in a sixteenth-century manuscript, the 'Guildford Book of Court'?

4. Who compiled the *Little Keyboard Book*, a set of pieces for his eldest son, Wilhelm Friedemann, to play?

5. In which country was the *Book of Durrow* written and illuminated?

6. Which Roman author wrote the great architectural treatise generally known in English as *The Ten Books of Architecture*?

7. From which artist did Étienne Chevalier commission illustrations for a book of hours, which became probably the artist's greatest work?

8. Which book guided German bombers in a campaign launched in 1942?

9. What very large-scale inventory was completed in England in 1087?

10. What name is given to the category of book left in Egyptian tombs, providing details that will be of use in the next world?

85

1. Which group of people returned to England in the 1650s after an absence of more than three centuries?

2. The longest novel in the English language consists of the correspondence of Clarissa Harlowe. Which author was guiding her pen?

3. Which mechanical contestant defeated two rivals in the Rainhill trials?

4. Who set up in the 1750s as an 'improver of grounds' and soon acquired a catchy nickname?

5. Who designed the Royal Pavilion in Brighton for the Prince Regent?

6. In memory of which fellow student at Cambridge did John Milton write *Lycidas*?

7. An English clergyman invented in the 1580s a machine to knit a useful commodity – what?

8. On what habit did James I launch a blistering attack, calling it a loathsome custom?

9. Between which two thriving cities did the first mail coaches begin to run in the 1780s?

10. Which bold concept by Joseph Paxton was constructed in London in just six months?

86

1. Which comedy by Oliver Goldsmith was first performed in London in 1773?

2. In which city did the shogun Yoshimitsu build a Golden Pavilion as his own villa?

3. Whose last completed novel was *The Golden Bowl*?

4. In which modern country was the first great American gold rush, in 1693?

5. Why did Bach's set of *Goldberg Variations*, published in 1741, acquire that name?

6. At which stockade did Australian gold-diggers make a defiant stand in 1854?

7. Which Swiss-born architect based his architectural unit, the Modulor, on the 'golden section'?

8. Which two kings met on the Field of Cloth of Gold?

9. What system of currency was formally adopted by Britain in the early nineteenth century and was finally abandoned in the 1930s?

10. Who wrote the opera *The Golden Cockerel*, which had its premiere in Moscow in 1909?

87

1. Who first attracted attention, with his partner, Gilbert, miming to Flanagan and Allen's 'Underneath the Arches'?

2. Which naval officer sailed from Britain in the 1790s, on a journey that would bring him to the north-west coast of America?

3. Which French novelist met Frédéric Chopin in the 1830s and lived with him for the next nine years?

4. Which English mathematician described a new form of algebra in his pamphlet *Mathematical Analysis of Logic*?

5. Which territory was granted in 1732 to a group of British philanthropists, to give a new start in life to debtors?

6. Which US secretary of state launched a generous and highly successful plan in 1948?

7. Which 25-year-old published a *Treatise Concerning the Principles of Human Knowledge*, attacking the philosophy of John Locke?

8. Who founded the American Institute of Public Opinion in the 1930s?

9. Who made, in the 1920s, the first records featuring his trademark ukulele?

10. Who demonstrated the advantages of alternating current when he provided 100,000 lights for the Chicago World's Fair?

88

1. What name was formally given to the new Christian city inaugurated in AD 330?

2. Which now-ruined city in Mongolia was the headquarters of Genghis Khan and was developed by his son Ogadai?

3. The fire department of which German city coined the term 'firestorm' to describe the unprecedented effects of an RAF raid in 1943?

4. Which great work of Christian philosophy did St Augustine write in response to the fall of Rome to the Visigoths?

5. In which of Charlie Chaplin's films does the tramp befriend a blind flower girl?

6. Which city, in the extreme south-east of Turkey, fell to the knights of the first crusade after a siege of seven months?

7. Which city did Shah Abbas I establish as a spectacular new Persian capital?

8. Which city rose and fell, according to the opera by Kurt Weill and Bertolt Brecht?

9. Which city did Napoleon find abandoned and burning after his victory at Borodino?

10. What type of contest was the City Dionysia in ancient Athens?

89

1. Who travelled from Rome to Athens in the first century AD to give some of his celebrated (or notorious) performances?

2. Which giants were believed to have built the massive stone architecture of Mycenaean towns such as Tiryns?

3. After an unbroken tradition of more than 1000 years, what annual event was brought to an abrupt end in AD 393?

4. Of what did Hipparchus make the first scientific catalogue?

5. From which German state did the newly independent Greece choose a prince to become its king?

6. Which living philosopher was satirized in *Clouds*, a comedy by Aristophanes?

7. Who sang her first Tosca in the opera house in Athens in 1941?

8. For which new building did Phidias sculpt a huge statue of Athena to be the central feature?

9. Whom did Philip II of Macedon employ as a tutor to his thirteen-year-old son?

10. Which nation responded with a classic case of gunboat diplomacy after Don Pacifico's house in Athens was burnt by an anti-Semitic mob?

90

1. Which philosopher's career, as a teacher at Notre-Dame, was brought to an abrupt end by scandal in the early twelfth century?

2. What was revived internationally by Pierre de Coubertin in the 1890s?

3. What was the name of the chamber ensemble formed in 1967 by British composers Harrison Birtwistle and Peter Maxwell Davies?

4. Where did a dramatic event, supposedly a surprise, happen on Christmas Day in the year 800?

5. Who began in 1968 an almost unbroken run of sixteen years as Canada's prime minister?

6. Who wrote *Illywhacker*, a novel narrated by a 139-year-old Australian?

7. Which composer was invited to London by the impresario Johann Peter Salomon?

8. Who began, in the 1640s, a seventeen-year spell as director-general of the Dutch colony of New Netherlands?

9. Pierre Schaeffer wrote the first examples of what type of music, in the 1940s, and coined the name of the genre?

10. Which book by Peter Read revealed the scandal of Aboriginal children forcibly removed from their parents?

91

1. Which class of animals were the first to master flight?

2. What was the name of the plane in which Charles Lindbergh flew solo across the Atlantic?

3. In which style of architecture did flying buttresses become a striking new feature of cathedrals?

4. In what type of aircraft did Otto Lilienthal make many pioneering flights in the 1890s?

5. Who was the first to fly across the English Channel, winning the £1000 prize offered by the *Daily Mail*?

6. Which two men were made much of when they arrived at Clifden, in Ireland, in 1919?

7. Who painted *Christ of St John of the Cross*, in which the crucified Christ seems to fly on his cross?

8. Which of two brothers was the first to make a successful powered flight of forty yards at Kitty Hawk in North Carolina?

9. Whose unusual circus was first seen on British TV in 1969?

10. Which entrepreneur, more commonly associated with the motor car, was the first to fly non-stop across the English Channel and back?

92

1. What resonant name was given by Camillo di Cavour to the newspaper that he launched in 1847, calling for an Italian nation?

2. Who won major awards with her second novel, *The Shipping News*?

3. What humorous weekly was founded by Harold Ross?

4. Which Russian exile published in London a radical newspaper called *Kolokol*, meaning 'the bell'?

5. What catchy slogan was coined by Adolph Ochs when he acquired *The New York Times* in 1897?

6. Which Indian tribe adopted an American-style constitution and published the first American-Indian newspaper?

7. News of what event on the property of John Sutter, on the Sacramento River, provoked a massive response?

8. Which English cartoonist had a fifty-year career in the nineteenth century with the satirical magazine *Punch*?

9. What was the name of the workers' newspaper first published before the First World War in St Petersburg and promising 'truth'?

10. What was the first of a new kind of journal, launched in the early eighteenth century for the customers in London's coffee houses?

93

1. After what event was the last Mughal emperor exiled by the British to Rangoon?

2. Which region of north-west Pakistan and eastern Afghanistan has given its name to a naturalistic style of Buddhist sculpture?

3. Which British officer held out against the Marathas and the French when besieged for seven weeks in the south Indian town of Arcot?

4. Herbert Baker was one of the architects providing new government buildings in Delhi early in the twentieth century. Who was the other?

5. Who served three long spells as prime minister after the assassination of the previous prime minister, her husband, in 1959?

6. What was Mahatma Gandhi protesting against in the 240-mile march that he led from Ahmedabad to the sea?

7. Whose arrest in East Pakistan provoked civil war in 1971?

8. What is the title of the Sanskrit epic that tells of the adventures of a prince, Rama of Ayodhya?

9. Who founded the Nirmal Hriday, or Kalighat Home for Dying Destitutes?

10. Which Persian ruler entered Delhi in the 1730s and removed much of the accumulated treasure of the Mughal empire?

94

1. Which massively successful novel by Harriet Beecher Stowe stirred up strong anti-slavery feeling in much of the USA?

2. Legislation abolishing the slave trade was passed in the same year in Britain and the USA – which year?

3. Which recently settled Portuguese islands were granted a monopoly on the new Atlantic slave trade in the mid fifteenth century?

4. What name, of great resonance ever since, was adopted by the anti-slavery party formed in the USA in the 1850s to oppose the Kansas–Nebraska Act?

5. In whose honour did Scottish missionaries in 1876 establish Blantyre, in modern Malawi, as a centre in the fight against slavery?

6. What balance was kept by the Missouri Compromise of 1820, which agreed that Maine and Missouri should both be admitted to the Union?

7. Which legal code gives an insight into Babylonian law and society, including the law relating to slaves?

8. What right was given to slave owners in Southern states by the Fugitive Slave Laws, passed by the US Congress in 1793?

9. Which island, settled by the British in the mid seventeenth century, soon became the major slave market of the Caribbean?

10. Which Amendment to the US Constitution prohibited slavery or any 'involuntary servitude' in the USA?

95

1. Which pianist became prime minister of the newly independent Poland in 1919?

2. Who wrote the *Manifesto* published by the newly founded Fabian Society?

3. Which nursery rhyme was chosen for the first recording that Thomas Edison made on his newly patented phonograph?

4. Who was elected the president of the newly formed Confederate States of America?

5. Which islands did the newly independent republic of Argentina immediately take possession of?

6. Who was elected chairman of the newly formed Polish trade union movement Solidarity?

7. In which newly formed corporation was the first programmable microchip designed?

8. Who designed the great tapestry that was hung above the altar in the newly consecrated Coventry cathedral in 1962?

9. Who became director of the newly formed Bauhaus, in Weimar?

10. Which sculptor and architect was given the task of adding baroque glamour to the newly completed St Peter's in Rome?

96

1. In terms of time span, what does Virginia Woolf's *Mrs Dalloway* have in common with James Joyce's *Ulysses*?

2. Which James Fenimore Cooper hero takes the side of a Mohican chief in a novel of the 1820s?

3. In which English school did Tom Brown spend his schooldays?

4. What was the name of the hunchback of Notre-Dame?

5. In what vehicle does James have bizarre adventures in a 1961 novel for children by Roald Dahl?

6. What name did Jack Kerouac give to his autobiographical novel about travelling through the USA and Mexico?

7. Of which fictional family are Franny and Zooey members?

8. Who was the Scarlet Pimpernel?

9. Whose autobiography was ghost-written by Robert Graves, nearly nineteen centuries after his death?

10. What was the name of the irrepressibly optimistic orphan created in the early twentieth century by Eleanor Porter?

97

1. Whose freedom of movement was limited in the Five Mile Act?

2. In which decade did Russia adopt its first Five-Year Plan?

3. Which Federal Act gave 160 acres in the west of the USA to any family farming them for five years?

4. In which Canadian family were five girls born in quick succession in the 1930s?

5. Where were Five Members conspicuously absent in the 1640s?

6. Which group did Enid Blyton introduce to the world when she took them to a treasure island in 1942?

7. What nickname did Calouste Gulbenkian acquire in about 1914 as a result of the oil deals he negotiated?

8. Of which religion are the five Ks the outward signs of membership?

9. What was extended in 472 BC to five days, of which the first and last were taken up with religious ceremonies?

10. What very significant development was first installed in the Haughwout Store, a five-storey building in New York?

98

1. In which town was North America's first university founded?

2. Whose journal of life in New England was published, much later, as *History of Plymouth Plantation*?

3. What is the name given to the historic engineering feat achieved at Coalbrookdale in 1779?

4. Who, together with Frederick Soddy, identified the phenomenon of radioactive half-life?

5. Of which town is Michael Henchard the mayor?

6. Who directed Marlon Brando and Martin Sheen in *Apocalypse Now*?

7. Which British artist was an influential pioneer in the development of op art?

8. Which was the first of two battles fought by Harold II in 1066?

9. Which university press began publishing the mighty *New English Dictionary* in 1884?

10. Where were James Stirling and Michael Wilford studying when they registered a famous domain name?

99

1. Who played the male lead in the film version of Tennessee Williams's play *Cat on a Hot Tin Roof*?

2. What name did Paul Scott give to his sequence of four novels that were later televised as *The Jewel in the Crown*?

3. To which established poet did the sixteen-year-old Arthur Rimbaud send some of his poems?

4. Whose Trinidad family features in *A House for Mr Biswas*?

5. Whose death enabled Adolf Hitler to combine the role of president with that of chancellor?

6. The capture of which fortress by the Bolsheviks gave them effective control of Petrograd?

7. Which evangelist and companion of St Paul on his final journey to Rome is thought to be the author of the Acts of the Apostles?

8. Who wrote the opera *Mathis der Maler*, which was banned by the Nazis?

9. Which Austrian theoretical physicist gave mathematical proof of the existence of the neutrino before it was identified?

10. With whose band did Bing Crosby make his first record, singing 'I've Got the Girl?

100

1. Which French physicist, better known for the lens that bears his name, published the theory that light is invariably a transverse wave?

2. For what device, tested in 1949 in Kazakhstan, did the Americans use the codename Joe One?

3. Who demonstrated the link between wavelength and colour in light?

4. Which physician to Queen Elizabeth I concluded that the earth is a magnet and coined the term 'magnetic pole'?

5. What did John Cockcroft and Ernest Walton achieve in the 1930s, by means of accelerated protons?

6. Which German physicist developed an instrument that could detect and count alpha particles?

7. Which Italian physicist led the team in Chicago that achieved the first nuclear chain reaction?

8. Who wrote to President Roosevelt in the late 1930s, warning of the potential of an atomic bomb?

9. Which Italian physicist described to London's Royal Society how his 'pile' of discs could produce electric current?

10. The French physicist Antoine Henri Becquerel was the first to discover natural radioactivity – in the salts of which element?

101

1. Which patriotic hymn by Samuel Francis Smith was sung for the first time one Fourth of July in Boston?

2. Songs by which US rock and roll band were used by Twyla Tharp for her ballet *Deuce Coupe*?

3. What was the nickname by which the French singer Edith Gassion became known, deriving from her diminutive size?

4. In which two cities was the Live Aid concert held simultaneously in the mid 1980s?

5. What stirring song did Rouget de Lisle write at short notice in the 1790s?

6. Who had a big hit with her first record, 'Downhearted Blues', selling two million copies within a year?

7. Who played piano in her husband's newly formed jazz band, the Hot Five?

8. Which eighteen-year-old had his first hit with 'Move It', at the start of a very long career?

9. What name for a new jazz style was featured for the first time on the label of a record by 'Pine Top' Smith in the 1920s?

10. What became the most popular song with patriot troops during the American Revolution?

102

1. Which large painting was first exhibited in the Spanish Pavilion at the World Fair in Paris?

2. The Paris workshops of which famous family were bought by Jean-Baptiste Colbert to become a royal factory for Louis XIV?

3. Which African-American singer was 'jazz hot' in La Revue Nègre in Paris?

4. Which romantic drama by Victor Hugo provoked a riot in the Paris audience on its first performance?

5. Which building in Paris was designed by Renzo Piano and Richard Rogers?

6. What is the name of René Clair's film about a Parisian street singer?

7. Which Parisian landmark was tightly bound in fabric by the US artist Christo?

8. What did French physicist Léon Foucault demonstrate in the Panthéon in Paris?

9. What was assembled in Paris in the 1880s before being shipped to America?

10. What influential new style in decorative art derived its name from a Paris exhibition of the 1920s?

103

1. Saddam Hussein was found hiding in a subterranean hole near which Iraqi town?

2. Where was Cola di Rienzo appointed tribune of the people, enjoying a few months of dictatorial power before the citizens tired of him?

3. Who succeeded Kim Il Sung as dictator in North Korea?

4. Who seized power in Athens in the mid sixth century BC and ruled for some thirty years as a benevolent dictator?

5. Which dictator of Panama was captured by US troops in the 1990s and taken to Miami on drug trafficking charges?

6. In which Caribbean republic did Rafael Trujillo establish a dictatorship that lasted for thirty years?

7. In which country did Juvenal Habyarimana win power in a military coup in 1973 and rule until his death in a plane crash twenty-one years later?

8. Who assumed dictatorial powers in Indonesia in the 1950s, operating a policy officially known as 'guided democracy'?

9. Which film was the first in which Charlie Chaplin spoke coherent dialogue?

10. Who arrived in Lima in the early 1820s and was granted dictatorial powers in the republic of Peru?

104

1. What was the name of the ship in which Robert Falcon Scott made his first voyage to the Antarctic?

2. What valuable commodity was discovered in large quantities at Potosi, in Bolivia?

3. Where were the first identified remains of Neanderthal man discovered in the 1850s?

4. What substance did Leo Baekeland discover in 1909, calling it 'the material of a thousand uses'?

5. What did a company formed by William Knox d'Arcy discover in Iran in 1908?

6. Which remote layer was discovered by French physicists Charles Fabry and Henri Buisson?

7. Who rightly believed that he had discovered the source of the Nile, when he reached Lake Victoria in the 1850s?

8. The secret of making what commodity was discovered in Dresden by Johann Friedrich Böttger?

9. The supposed remains of which saint were discovered in Spain at Compostela, turning it into a major new centre of pilgrimage?

10. What discovery did the followers of Pythagoras make about the octave?

105

1. In which city did Charles I establish his court during the English Civil War?

2. Who was appointed court painter to the new Spanish king Charles IV?

3. In the court theatre of which ruler did Mozart's opera *Così fan Tutte* have its premiere?

4. Who is now by far the best known of those who sat for a portrait bust by the court sculptor Thutmose?

5. In the court of which country did Crown Prince Dipendra kill nine members of his own family?

6. Which far from modest home did Cardinal Wolsey build for himself but later give to Henry VIII?

7. At the court theatre in which city did Wagner's opera *Tristan and Isolde* have its premiere?

8. Which Italian artist did the Holy Roman Emperor Charles V makes his court painter in the 1530s?

9. Which artist moved to London in the 1630s and rapidly became the favourite portrait painter of the court and aristocracy?

10. What name was given to the court museum that Catherine the Great established as an extension of the Winter Palace?

106

1. Who, though in possession of a first-class ticket, was forcibly ejected from a railway carriage in Pietermaritzburg?

2. What name, meaning 'migrating farmers', was given to Dutch nomads moving north from Cape Town?

3. Of which tribal group was Shaka the ruler?

4. Which European congress assigned the Cape of Good Hope finally to Britain?

5. In which country did UNITA engage in a civil war lasting twenty-seven years?

6. Which town has developed from a settlement established originally by Jan van Riebeck?

7. Which European navigator was the first to sail his ship round the Cape of Good Hope?

8. Who shared the Nobel Peace Prize in 1993?

9. What did Dutch settlers begin calling themselves in the late eighteenth century, to emphasize their new identity?

10. Which leader of ZAPU was defeated by Robert Mugabe in the first election in independent Zimbabwe?

107

1. Who was sent from Germany in the 1840s to manage his family's cotton-spinning factory in Manchester?

2. Who opened a small shop selling millinery in Deauville just before the First World War and went on to become an international name in female fashion?

3. Ships of which nation gathered each year at Portobelo, bringing in home-produced goods and preparing to take back metal?

4. Britain's first Factory Act limited a child's working day in a factory to how many hours?

5. Which oasis city in northern Syria became wealthy in Roman times through being on the caravan route between Mesopotamia and the Mediterranean?

6. What name did the English textile magnate Titus Salt give to the model industrial village he built for his workers?

7. Which area was the tsar Paul I planning to develop when he established the Russian–American Company?

8. In the 1880s, US entrepreneur James 'Buck' Duke won exclusive rights to a machine that could manufacture 100,000 items a day – what items?

9. In 1903, the USA was granted exclusive control in perpetuity of a valuable ten-mile corridor – where?

10. Which people counted the cedars of Lebanon among their most valuable exports, from the tenth century BC?

108

1. What was the name of the band, formed by Bob Marley and five others, that first gave Jamaican music a global following?

2. Who scored 501 runs when playing cricket for Warwickshire against Durham?

3. Which Antiguan author's first novel was *Annie John*?

4. In which harbour was the US battleship *Maine* blown up, sparking the Spanish–American War?

5. Which president was twice forced to flee from Haiti?

6. With which volunteer regiment of cavalry did Theodore Roosevelt fight against the Spanish in Cuba?

7. Which now-famous poet and playwright founded, in the 1950s, the Trinidad Theatre Workshop?

8. Where was Cuba forced, from the early twentieth century, to accept a permanent US military presence?

9. In which Caribbean island did the Rastafarian cult evolve?

10. Which president won and kept power supported by the brutal Tontons Macoutes?

109

1. What newly discovered technique did the Scottish obstetrician James Simpson use in the 1840s to ease difficult births?

2. The German surgeon Georg Clemens Perthes discovered early in the twentieth century a treatment that had the effect of inhibiting cancer – what treatment?

3. Which New Zealand surgeon was a pioneer in plastic surgery, publishing the textbook *Plastic Surgery of the Face*?

4. Of what was Louise Brown the first, in the 1970s?

5. Who, in the 1480s, began an unprecedented series of detailed anatomical drawings, based on corpses dissected in Rome?

6. What group concept was introduced by Carl Jung after his break with Sigmund Freud?

7. Who, early in the twentieth century, identified a new disease by studying the brain of a dead woman who had had presenile dementia?

8. What surgical technique, now increasingly in demand, was pioneered in the sixth century BC by the Indian surgeon Susruta?

9. What cause and effect, in terms of public health, were linked in a report commissioned by the British Medical Research Council in the early 1950s?

10. Which French surgeon, the greatest of his day, published in 1545 an influential account of how to treat gunshot wounds?

110

1. Who received wide publicity for putting love above duty in 1936?

2. Who wrote the novel *Love in the Time of Cholera*?

3. Who fell in love when he glimpsed Laura in a church in Avignon?

4. Which music-hall singer had a great success with his recording of 'I Love a Lassie'?

5. Which twenty-year-old Chilean poet became famous with the publication of his *Twenty Love Poems*?

6. For what had love been learnt in the subtitle of Stanley Kubrick's film *Dr Strangelove*?

7. Which heroine develops a fatal love for Count Vronsky?

8. Which Roman poet had an early success with a collection of witty love poems entitled simply *Amores*?

9. Which English parson, with a consuming love of food and wine, began to keep a diary in the 1750s?

10. What was the name of Lady Chatterley's lover?

III

1. The *Rigveda* is the earliest literature in which language?

2. Who performed in Cape Town a famous operation on Louis Washkansky?

3. Of which religion was Nanak the first guru?

4. Which town in Iran became, under the Mongols, the first centre of Persian miniature painting?

5. What does AUC stand for in Roman chronology?

6. Who paid for the first publication of *The Tale of Peter Rabbit*?

7. In what sense was the Suffragan Bishop of Massachusetts, consecrated in 1988, the first?

8. Which religion produced the world's first surviving printed book, from the ninth century?

9. What was the title of Lucy Maud Montgomery's first novel, which brought her immediate success?

10. Of what substance does the first known description appear in a Chinese manual of about 1040?

112

1. In which Asian country was the first type foundry established, casting movable type in bronze?

2. Which English ironmaster patented a process for puddling iron that produced a purer metal?

3. What is the name given to the bronze Buddha at Kamakura, in Japan?

4. Which British artist developed in the 1960s a style of welding and painting abstract metal sculpture?

5. The famous bronze sculptures of Benin are, in fact, made of another metal – which?

6. What is the English title of the first novel by the German author Günter Grass?

7. Where in Britain was a rich hoard of Roman silver discovered in 1942?

8. In which Caribbean island did the steel-band tradition first develop?

9. What source of metal was used when the highest British medal for valour, the Victoria Cross, was introduced?

10. What name has been given to the type of handwriting learnt, from the sixteenth century, from examples on engraved plates?

113

1. Which valuable island, extremely close to mainland India, did the Portuguese acquire by force in 1534 from the local ruler?

2. Which island was ruled by the Knights of St John as their own sovereign state in the fourteenth and fifteenth centuries?

3. Who cast a satirical eye on human society in his novel *L'Île des Pingouins* (*Penguin Island*)?

4. Which two authors made an expedition together to the western islands of Scotland in the eighteenth century?

5. On which Greek island was an armless statue of Aphrodite found, subsequently seen as an ideal of female beauty?

6. Which American state was founded by Roger Williams as a colony based on the principle of religious tolerance?

7. By what alternative name did the Moluccas become known, because of a lucrative trade?

8. What object, famous in history, was built on the island of Pharos?

9. Who, after being welcomed by the Huron Indians, gave their island in the St Lawrence River the name of Montreal?

10. What is the best-known feature of Bedloe's Island?

114

1. Where in the New World did colonists establish the first lasting British settlement?

2. What new word, meaning 'treatment by something similar', was coined by Samuel Hahnemann in 1796 to describe his new approach to medicine?

3. What new and badly needed system of calculation was introduced by Julius Caesar?

4. Which opera was commissioned from Verdi by the management of the new Cairo Opera House?

5. What catchy new song of 1895 was written by Banjo Paterson to music by Christina Macpherson?

6. Who is now by far the best known of the four new yeomen of the chamber employed by Edward III in 1367?

7. On what sacred spot did Herod build a new Temple for the Jews?

8. Who designed London's new Houses of Parliament, on which work began in the first year of Queen Victoria's reign?

9. Who became the first prime minister of the new Union of South Africa?

10. Who was given the task of providing London with a new system of sewers in the mid nineteenth century?

115

1. Which prime minister finally took Britain into the European Community?

2. Which suspension bridge was, in the 1980s and 1990s, the longest in the world?

3. Which iconic London site was bombed by the IRA, ending the fifteen-month ceasefire that had followed the Downing Street Declaration?

4. Who is the only British prime minister to have been assassinated?

5. Which British group in 1996 sold millions of their first album, breaking all previous UK records?

6. From a match in which city was the Manchester United football team returning when their plane crashed, killing eight players?

7. The imposition of what kind of tax sparked the Peasants' Revolt in the fourteenth century?

8. Which two staple foods, freely available during the Second World War, were rationed for the first time in 1946?

9. What did the Anglican vicar Chad Varah set up, using the crypt of a London church for his first branch?

10. Which work by Benjamin Britten, setting poems by Wilfred Owen, was first performed in the recently rebuilt Coventry Cathedral?

116

1. Which bascule bridge in London functioned for the first time in 1894?

2. Which Anglo-French project underwent its first significant test in 1969?

3. From what material was Britain's Mosquito constructed in the Second World War?

4. Of what did Igor Sikorsky develop the first practical example, in the 1930s?

5. What project linking Wapping and Rotherhithe did the Brunel engineers, father and son, complete in the 1840s?

6. Which engineer was appointed director of Germany's weapon research centre at Peenemünde in the 1930s?

7. Of what revolutionary kind of engine did Felix Wankel build a model in the 1920s, thirty years before the first prototype was manufactured?

8. Which great dam was completed on the Colorado River in the 1930s?

9. Which span of water, more than a mile wide, was crossed by a vast cantilever bridge in the 1890s?

10. Which Russian First World War pilot began a distinguished career as an aircraft designer in the 1920s?

117

1. Who caused offence in Muslim countries when he described the war on terror as a 'crusade'?

2. What triumphal two-word banner appeared on a US aircraft carrier in May 2003?

3. From which adventure were the Byzantine treasures of St Mark's brought back to Venice as loot?

4. Which saint, the first missionary of the Counter-Reformation, set sail from Lisbon to Goa in the 1540s?

5. What pact did a British military mission to Moscow hope to agree with Stalin in 1939?

6. Which crusade was provoked by the murder of the pope's legate to Toulouse in the early thirteenth century?

7. Which Italian poet turned the First Crusade into a romantic epic in his poem *Gerusalemme Liberata* (*Jerusalem Liberated*)?

8. Which Catholic order provided the missionaries sent to England during Elizabeth I's reign, Edmund Campion among them?

9. On what specific mission did Garnet Wolseley sail from London in the 1880s?

10. Which crusade began unpromisingly after the waters of the Mediterranean failed to part for the crusaders?

118

1. What was the title of the book in which Lytton Strachey combined brief biographies of four nineteenth-century figures?

2. Which US tennis player was the first to achieve the grand slam, winning the men's singles title in all four major tournaments in the same year?

3. Which British liner set four new records for crossing the Atlantic in the early twentieth century?

4. As what is the year AD 69 notorious in Roman history?

5. In what does 'Burnt Norton' form one of four?

6. Which was the last film that the Marx brothers made as a foursome?

7. What visionary group of four was defined by President F. D. Roosevelt in a speech to Congress in 1941?

8. Which orchestral work of the 1920s, by an American composer, has parts for four taxi-horns?

9. In what sense were Yao, Jiang, Zhang and Wang a group?

10. Which US golfer was the first man to achieve four victories in the British Open?

119

1. What colour accompanied black in a police context in Ireland after the First World War?

2. Which animal combines with black in the name of a party founded in Oakland, California, to campaign more aggressively for civil rights?

3. What was the first alternative to black in the new commodities introduced in Britain by Rowland Hill?

4. What combines with white in one of the most famous products of Delft?

5. What features with black in the title of an artist's 'arrangement' depicting his mother?

6. What colour was opposed to white in a fifteenth-century battle at St Albans?

7. In which South American country were the rival followers of Rivera and Oribe known as the Reds and the Whites?

8. What colour did Kasimir Malevich combine with white in a famous series of paintings after the First World War?

9. What colour is found with black in the title of Rebecca West's classic account of Yugoslavia?

10. Where did President Taft combine white with oval in the early twentieth century?

120

1. Which Austrian painter was sent briefly to prison for some highly explicit images of nudes?

2. Whom did Michael Collins spring from Lincoln Gaol, with the help of a duplicate key?

3. Whose son was the tsarevitch Alexis, who died from violence inflicted on him in one of his father's prisons?

4. Who was sharing Adolf Hitler's prison cell when the writing of *Mein Kampf* was begun?

5. To which prison was Oscar Wilde sent to serve a two-year sentence with hard labour?

6. Who was by far the most distinguished of those taken prisoner by the Germans at the Battle of Sedan?

7. In which country was Paul Verlaine put in prison, after wounding Arthur Rimbaud with a gunshot in a drunken rage?

8. Which US painter made his name with a Civil War subject, *Prisoners from the Front*?

9. Which king was imprisoned after being recognized in an inn near Vienna, on his way home from the Holy Land?

10. Which forbidding fortress held just seven prisoners when they were liberated by an excited Paris mob?

121

1. Which film, based on a play by Eugene O'Neill, was featured as 'Garbo talks' and broke all previous box-office records?

2. Which British racing driver set a new water speed record of 141 mph in the 1930s?

3. Which art deco skyscraper in New York held the record as the world's tallest, but only for a year?

4. Who scored a record 344 runs in the 1870s, playing for the Marylebone Cricket Club against Kent at Canterbury?

5. Which 21-year-old set a still unbroken record, pitching thirteen successive scoreless innings, in his first World Series for the Boston Red Sox?

6. What powered the car in which Leon Serpollet set a new land speed record of 75 mph along the Promenade des Anglais in Nice in 1902?

7. Who completed, in 1967, a record involving nearly 30,000 miles and more than 200 days?

8. Which US industrialist set a new speed record of 352 mph in the 1930s, flying a plane of his own design?

9. Which US singer created a new record when her fourth successive album went straight to the top of the Billboard 200?

10. Which US athlete set a world long-jump record that stood for twenty-three years?

122

1. What was the name of the US nuclear power station that suffered partial meltdown?

2. Who made three ineffectual attempts to invade England before being captured by Henry VII and hanged at Tyburn?

3. Which US swimmer won three gold medals in the 1924 Paris Olympics?

4. Which was the first of the three 'spaghetti westerns' directed by Sergio Leone?

5. Which sisters sold only two copies when they jointly published a collection of their poems in 1846?

6. Who caused a sensation with the grotesque creatures in his *Three Studies for Figures at the Base of a Crucifixion*?

7. What name is given to the system of crop rotation introduced by the Franks in about AD 850?

8. Which British tennis player won three consecutive singles titles at Wimbledon between the wars?

9. Who died, with three of his sons, during or as a result of a battle on Mount Gilboa?

10. What name is given to the parliament dismissed by Charles I after only three weeks?

123

1. In which century was Wales merged with England as a principality?

2. Whose 'play for voices' was broadcast with Richard Burton as the narrator?

3. When the Welsh rose against the English at the start of the fifteenth century, whom did they proclaim as their own Prince of Wales?

4. Who was returned to Parliament in the early twentieth century as the Member for Merthyr Tydfil, forging a close link between the Labour Party and Wales?

5. The word 'Welsh' derives from the Anglo-Saxon name for them, *wealas*. What did it mean?

6. Which Welsh poet had a great success with *The Autobiography of a Super-Tramp*?

7. Where did a sliding slag heap in Wales bury a village school, killing 116 children?

8. Which party was founded in a temperance hotel in Pwllheli during a National Eisteddfod?

9. Which game did Major Walter Wingield develop at his home in Wales, taking out a patent for it under the name Sphairistike?

10. Near which Welsh iron-working town was the world's first locomotive on rails established by Richard Trevithick?

124

1. Who painted *Ennui*, depicting a difficult or dreary moment in a marriage?

2. Who was the object in the sentence: 'Reader, I married him'?

3. Who married Saskia van Uylenburgh, who features in many of his paintings?

4. Which star of which sport did Marilyn Monroe marry as her second husband?

5. For whom was the law changed to allow him, though of senatorial rank, to marry Theodora, whom courtesy describes as an actress?

6. Which composer was the father of Richard Wagner's wife Cosima?

7. At the wedding of which couple was Joseph Goebbels the principal guest, in the spring of 1945?

8. Who married Catherine von Bora, a former nun?

9. With which opera did Glyndebourne open its very first season, in the 1930s?

10. Which US sculptor married the Italian porn star La Cicciolina?

125

1. Which place did Grand Prince Yaroslav develop in the eleventh century as his capital city, providing it with spectacular Christian churches?

2. What instruction did Lenin intend to give the Communist Party in his Testament, but was prevented from doing so?

3. Who died of pneumonia in the station master's house at Astapovo?

4. What was the origin of the tribes known as the Rus, who established themselves as traders around Novgorod in the ninth century?

5. Of which better-known organization was the Cheka the origin?

6. Which two politicians, from the US and the USSR, engaged in a much publicized 'kitchen debate' in Moscow?

7. Which two Soviet republics joined with Belarus to declare independence from the USSR, thus effectively breaking up the Union?

8. Who died from a stomach wound received in a duel with his brother-in-law?

9. Whose semi-autobiographical novel *Notes from the House of the Dead* describes life in a Siberian labour camp?

10. Who courageously foiled a hard-line Communist coup in Moscow in 1991?

126

1. Whose code of behaviour was known as *Bushido*?

2. What Japanese phrase, an abbreviation of the words for 'empty orchestra', became famous around the world from the 1960s?

3. What title was given to Yoritomo in the twelfth century, as the first of many officials in this post who were more powerful than their emperors?

4. What was the message that the emperor Hirohito had for his people, on the first occasion that they heard his voice?

5. What Japanese sedentary game is held to have been introduced from China in the eighth century?

6. What name was given to the pact agreed by Japan and Germany in the 1930s against their perceived common enemy?

7. Which English artist discovered his future craft at a raku party in Japan, where each guest was invited to throw a pot?

8. Which Chinese state was occupied by the Japanese in the early 1930s?

9. Who created a famous series of colour-printed views of Mount Fuji?

10. What phrase is used to describe the delights of the entertainment areas of Edo and Kyoto?

127

1. Which American novelist moved to London in 1876, but lived his last years in Sussex?

2. Which Russian-born architect set up the modernist firm of Tecton in London in 1932?

3. Who made his home in London after being expelled from Germany in 1848, Europe's year of revolutions?

4. Which Polish dancer opened in London, in 1920, a famous ballet school that still survives?

5. Which son of J. S. Bach moved to London in 1762 and became known as the English Bach?

6. Which American rapidly became Britain's most fashionable portrait-painter after moving to London in 1885?

7. Who decided to settle in London after the success of his opera *Rinaldo* in 1711?

8. Which US entrepreneur opened the first British custom-built department store in London's Oxford Street?

9. Which American sculptor moved from New York to settle in London in 1905?

10. Which Russian ballerina settled in London in 1911 and formed her own touring company?

128

1. Which Norwegian figure skater won gold medals in three successive Olympic Games, beginning in the 1920s?

2. Which two antagonists agreed the Oslo Accords brokered by the Norwegian government?

3. Who won five consecutive singles titles at Wimbledon, from the mid 1970s?

4. At which battle in Scandinavian waters did Horatio Nelson put his telescope to his blind eye?

5. The death of which Swedish king inspired an opera by Verdi?

6. Which kingdom was united by Harold Bluetooth in the tenth century?

7. How did Tollund Man die?

8. Which dynasty began with the seizing of the throne by Gustavus I in 1523?

9. Who sailed into the Arctic in the purpose-built *Fram*, beginning a three-year attempt to reach the North Pole?

10. Which Danish physicist used quantum theory as a key to understanding the structure of the atom?

129

1. Which museum, with a striking design by Frank Gehry, opened to great acclaim in 1997?

2. What spectacular buildings, designed by Werner March, were completed in 1936?

3. Where is there a famous glass pyramid by Ieoh Ming Pei?

4. Which famous school of modern art and architecture did the Nazis close down in 1933?

5. Of what famous building was Ictinos the architect?

6. Who designed Fallingwater in Mill Run, Pennsylvania?

7. What German name was used by an association of architects, designers and industrialists formed in Munich in 1907?

8. Which striking building in New York, no longer in existence, was designed by Minoru Yamasaki?

9. In which city did Adolf Loos design the Steiner House in the beginnings of the modernist style?

10. For what new town did work begin in 1767, to the design of the 23-year-old James Craig?

130

1. Which two units merged to form a single kingdom, defined now as the start of the First Dynasty?

2. Which two Middle East leaders shared the Nobel Peace Prize in 1978?

3. Who led the group of officers that deposed the Egyptian king Farouk?

4. With which country did Egypt merge briefly as the United Arab Republic?

5. Why is the Rosetta Stone so named?

6. Which great Muslim leader deposed the Fatimid caliph of Egypt in the twelfth century?

7. What is Howard Carter's main claim to fame?

8. Where did Ramses II create a spectacular temple in his own honour?

9. Who won control of Egypt in the late fourth century BC, inaugurating the final dynasty?

10. In which city were 300 Mameluke guests of the viceroy Muhammad Ali assassinated during a banquet?

131

1. Who created Auguste Dupin, who solved the mystery of the murders in the Rue Morgue in the 1840s?

2. In which novel did the hard-boiled Philip Marlowe first ply his trade?

3. Who applied his skills for the first time in *The Mysterious Affair at Styles*?

4. Which poet, doubling as a detective, was introduced by an English author in her first novel, in 1962?

5. Whose innocence was stressed in the title of the novel in which he first appeared, in the early twentieth century?

6. In which novel did James Bond first feature?

7. Which gentleman detective made his first appearance in *Whose Body?*, in the 1920s?

8. Who first appeared in *Pietr-le-Letton*, published in the 1930s?

9. Who solved his first case in *The Maltese Falcon*?

10. Who made her first appearance in *Murder at the Vicarage*?

132

1. Which novel by Nathaniel Hawthorne is based on a curse supposedly invoked against his own family?

2. Which film by Akira Kurosawa is set in the warring states period in Japanese history?

3. Which English borough had in 1831 just seven voters but returned two members to Parliament in Westminster?

4. Who retired from competition after a seventh successive victory in the Tour de France?

5. Which two countries fought each other in the Northern Seven Years War?

6. By what name is Shostakovich's *Seventh Symphony* also known?

7. How many Anglo-Saxon kingdoms survived to form what became known as the Heptarchy?

8. Which was the first animated feature film?

9. What identifying characteristic had the seven women whose throats were slit in London's Whitechapel area by Jack the Ripper?

10. Which general led the Confederate side in the Seven Days Battles?

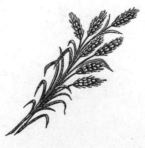

133

1. The first feature film by Jean-Luc Godard was a classic of French New Wave cinema. What was its title?

2. Who was assassinated in a Paris street by François Ravaillac?

3. Which composer established IRCAM, an advanced institute in Paris for research into the techniques of modern music?

4. Who, beginning an extremely varied career in diplomacy and politics, started in the 1770s by becoming an abbot at the age of twenty-one?

5. In which city and decade were thugs encouraged to massacre some 1400 aristocrats and priests being held in prisons?

6. Which character, created by Goscinny and Uderzo, made his first appearance in the magazine *Pilote* in the 1950s?

7. Who, in the 1720s, painted the most splendid shop sign in history, for his friend Gersaint?

8. What all-embracing title did Honoré de Balzac give to the collected edition of his fiction that he began publishing in the 1840s?

9. Which jazz guitarist and violinist together formed the Quintette du Hot Club de France in the 1930s?

10. Which brilliant French chemist was guillotined for having been involved with tax collection during the *ancien régime*?

134

1. What name did Robert J. Flaherty give to his dramatized documentary about the life of the Inuit in the Arctic?

2. In which church is the chapel designed by Robert Lorimer for the Knights of the Thistle?

3. What was used in Robert A. Millikan's famous experiment to determine the charge of an electron?

4. What is the title of the influential socialist novel written by Robert Tressell and published after his death?

5. Which song of Bob Dylan's featured in his album *The Freewheelin' Bob Dylan*, but had already been released by Peter, Paul and Mary?

6. Where was the mill that Robert Owen developed as an experiment in paternalistic socialism?

7. During which war was the Hungarian photographer Robert Capa killed in Vietnam?

8. What is the name of the nearest star to earth, discovered by Robert Innes at the Johannesburg Observatory?

9. What was the title of the single released by Bob Geldof and Band Aid to raise money for famine in Ethiopia?

10. Which drunken farmer has an alarming encounter with witches in a poem by Robert Burns?

135

1. Where in Spain did the young daughter of an amateur archaeologist discover the first known examples of prehistoric art?

2. Fossilized bones of what species have been significant finds in the caves of Skhul and Qafzeh in modern Israel?

3. Where in India, near Aurangabad, is there a group of Buddhist, Hindu and Jain cave temples carved in elaborate detail from the rock?

4. Which sect hid their sacred scrolls in caves near the Dead Sea, to save them from the Romans?

5. Where in Dublin was the Irish chief secretary, Lord Frederick Cavendish, assassinated?

6. Which nurse was court-martialled and executed by German forces in Belgium?

7. At which oasis on the Silk Road are there as many as 500 caves decorated with Buddhist murals?

8. Which English chemist isolated hydrogen but believed that it was phlogiston?

9. Which cave inspired Felix Mendelssohn on a visit to the Hebrides in 1829?

10. Which cave in southern France, with the world's oldest known paintings, was discovered only in the 1990s?

136

1. The existence of what was discovered by English physicist Joseph John Thomson, working at the Cavendish laboratory in Cambridge?

2. What is St Helena, the mother of the Roman emperor Constantine, supposed to have discovered in Jerusalem?

3. What discovery, of alarming significance, was announced in 1939 by a team of German physicists led by Otto Hahn?

4. What dimension, of importance in apiculture, was discovered by an American clergyman, L. L. Langstroth?

5. The principle of what instrument was discovered by Italian physicist Evangelista Torricelli when he observed variations in a column of mercury?

6. Which discovery by US physicists Arno Penzias and Robert Wilson lent strong support to the Big Bang theory?

7. What harmful bacillus was discovered by the German bacteriologist Robert Koch?

8. Which Assyrian city did British archaeologist Henry Layard discover in his first month of digging in Iraq?

9. What was observed by Marcello Malpighi, making clear for the first time how blood circulates around the human body?

10. What aspect of the human body was discovered by the Austrian biochemist Karl Landsteiner?

137

1. What act, in disregard of the rules, was performed by the schoolboy William Webb Ellis in the founding myth of a modern sport?

2. With what virus did Edward Jenner inoculate a boy, in a pioneering experiment of the 1790s?

3. In what film, directed by Ang Lee, did two Wyoming cowboys develop a homosexual relationship?

4. Which US poet's first book of poems had the title *A Boy's Will*?

5. Which group's *Licensed to Ill* became the first rap, or hip hop, album to top the US chart?

6. Of what species is the Turkana Boy the most complete known skeleton?

7. Who wrote the novel *A Suitable Boy*, a family saga set in post-independence India?

8. Peter the Great trimmed the beards of which reactionary group, in a gesture of reform?

9. What name did Richard Wright give to his account of his early life in Mississippi and then Chicago?

10. Boys of what religion were trained to become members of the elite corps of janissaries?

138

1. Which historic city in Iran was destroyed early in the present century by a massive earthquake?

2. What is the name of Firdausi's great chronicle of Persian history?

3. In which embassy did supporters of Ayatollah Khomeini seize sixty-six hostages?

4. Where did Darius I build a new palace and capital in the late sixth century BC?

5. Which dynasty was established by Reza Khan after he mounted a coup to depose the ruling Qaja shah?

6. Which Iranian prophet preached that there was only one god, Ahura Mazda?

7. What was the origin of the Il-khans, who ruled Persia after invading the country in 1256?

8. In which of the Persian arts did Bihzad excel?

9. Which Iranian prime minister was removed from office in an armed coup sponsored by the CIA and Britain's MI6?

10. What hereditary title did the shah of Persia grant to the leader of the Ismaili sect?

139

1. To what meteorological feature did Shelley, while in Italy, write an ode?

2. Which English poet developed the new verse form that he called 'sprung rhythm'?

3. Which American poet had only six poems published in her lifetime but six volumes published from the papers found after her death?

4. Which moralizing verses by Rudyard Kipling, published before the First World War, rapidly became his most popular poem with the British public?

5. Which epic Middle English poem has a narrator who calls himself Will and is attributed to William Langland?

6. What river did Roger McGough, Brian Patten and Adrian Henri include in the title of their joint anthology in the 1960s?

7. Which thirteenth-century poet described the new form of poetry being written in his time as a sweet new style, or *dolce stil nuovo*?

8. Which much-reissued collection by Walt Whitman grew from just twelve poems in 1855 to two fat volumes in the US centennial year of 1876?

9. Which poem, by now his most famous, did William Blake include in the preface to his book *Milton*?

10. To which Old English poem did the Irish author Seamus Heaney bring many new readers through a new translation published in the 1990s?

140

1. What was the previous name of the group that became the Six Nations when the Tuscarora joined?

2. The first of six had six children, only one of whom survived to inherit a crown. Who was the mother in question?

3. Which choir was established by Pope Sixtus IV?

4. What territory did Israel capture from Syria in the Six Day War?

5. Which free-thinking Holy Roman Emperor, leading the Sixth Crusade, briefly recovered Jerusalem by negotiating with the Muslims?

6. Six members of which gang were murdered by rival gangsters on St Valentine's Day?

7. In which dynasty did a Chinese emperor have the six main Confucian classics inscribed in stone, so that scholars could take rubbings?

8. In which country did six composers become famous as a group after the First World War?

9. Which British golfer holds a record, now almost a century old, of six victories in Britain's Open championship?

10. From what village did the six farm labourers come who were transported to Australia for administering unlawful oaths?

141

1. In which German city were the first watches made, soon known as 'eggs' because of their shape?

2. What was the three-word slogan used by Otto von Bismarck to describe the only policy by which he believed Prussia would become strong?

3. Who joined Wittenberg University to teach Greek and inspired Martin Luther to translate the Greek New Testament into German?

4. Which composer turned Oscar Wilde's play *Salome* into an opera?

5. What name was given to the German equivalents of the French troubadours, one example being Tannhäuser?

6. Which physicist observed, and drew, dark lines in the solar spectrum?

7. To which city did Christopher Isherwood say goodbye in the title of a novel?

8. Where was the so-called Battle of the Nations fought during the Napoleonic Wars?

9. Which philosopher published three 'critiques', the first of which was *The Critique of Pure Reason*?

10. What name did Frederick the Great give to the summer palace he built at Potsdam?

142

1. Which Caribbean hero was treacherously arrested in the early nineteenth century, and died in a French prison?

2. The bones of which two men were brought back to Melbourne in 1862 after a heroic failure to cross Australia?

3. Which author sent his hero, Tony Last, to a disastrous fate in the Amazon rain forest?

4. Who created an early anti-hero in his novel *L'Étranger*?

5. Which poet gave a military disaster a veneer of heroism in 1854?

6. Who became a national hero for his defence of Verdun but twenty-nine years later was seen as a national disgrace?

7. What action by Napoleon caused Beethoven to revise his opinion of his erstwhile hero?

8. Which sordid organization did Thomas Dixon present in heroic terms in *The Clansman*?

9. Which poem turned a minor military disaster for Charlemagne into a tale of epic heroism by one of his paladins?

10. Which hero of Philip Roth's reveals an unheroic private life when he describes his sexual frustrations to his psychiatrist, Dr Spielvogel?

143

1. Which inventor created, at Menlo Park in New Jersey, what he called his 'invention factory'?

2. What kind of vehicle was first successfully tested by French inventor Nicolas-Joseph Cugnot in the eighteenth century?

3. What device was added to personal computers for the first time in a new version of the Apple, launched in 1983?

4. What new writing material is traditionally supposed to have been invented by a Chinese eunuch, Ts'ai Lun?

5. Who invented a safety lamp that shielded the naked flame so as to avoid explosions in mines?

6. In what sense did a German physiologist, Adolf Fick, grind a pair of lenses in the 1880s for the uniquely personal needs of just one patient?

7. Who, in Philadelphia in 1838, demonstrated his greatly improved version of the electric telegraph?

8. What essential scientific instrument was first made in the late sixteenth century by Zacharias Janssen, a Dutch spectacle maker?

9. In the development of what scientific facility was ENIAC, built immediately after the Second World War, a significant step forward?

10. The world's earliest known striking clock is still in use and working today – in which building?

144

1. Which port in the Persian Gulf was seized by British forces in 1914 to protect the supply of Persian oil?

2. Which country's prime minister suffered in 2006 a massive stroke that left him in a coma?

3. What major undertaking was the emperor Frederick Barbarossa engaged in when he was drowned in a Turkish river?

4. Who is said in the Bible to have left Ur to move north with his tribe and flocks towards Canaan nearly 4000 years ago?

5. What name is given, in English, to the Turkish revolutionaries who organized an uprising in Salonika in 1908 against Ottoman autocracy?

6. Which nation invaded western Turkey after the First World War but met stiff and successful resistance?

7. What position, and what fate, was shared in sequence by Omar, Othman and Ali?

8. In which region was the Haganah set up as an underground military organization in the 1920s?

9. Which was the first centre of Mesopotamian civilization?

10. Navigators from which European nation seized Hormuz, in the early sixteenth century, to establish a garrison in the Gulf of Oman?

145

1. Which American states are represented by the first two extra stars added to the original thirteen on the Stars and Stripes?

2. Which were the remaining two tribes of Israel, after the ten tribes of northern Israel had been overwhelmed by the Assyrians?

3. Who provided two large paintings, *La Danse* and *La Musique*, for the staircase of Sergei Shchukin's house in Moscow?

4. Who invaded Britain on two separate occasions?

5. Which US author had immediate success with his book *Two Years before the Mast*, about his time as a merchant seaman?

6. Which church had a royal funeral and two coronations within a year of its consecration?

7. Who developed the theme of a new Conservatism uniting the 'two nations' of rich and poor?

8. What was limited to two by the Twenty-Second Amendment to the US Constitution?

9. In which European country were the two main political parties in the early eighteenth century known as the Hats and the Caps?

10. Which two kingdoms were merged in 1707?

146

1. What book did the tenth Sikh guru, Gobind Rai, name as his successor?

2. Whose long sleep was described in Washington Irving's 1820 *Sketch Book*?

3. What book about meat, eggs, sugar and tea could be found in every family home in Britain in 1940?

4. Who provided the English text for the new Anglican Church's Book of Common Prayer?

5. Of what Chinese religion is the title of the holy book usually translated as *The Way and the Power*?

6. Which Roman emperor differed considerably from others in writing twelve books of philosophical *Meditations*?

7. In which city did Euclid write what was for centuries Europe's standard textbook on geometry?

8. Which famous bloke made his first appearance in a 1915 book of poems by Australian author C. J. Dennis?

9. What very successful book did Old Possum put together just before the Second World War?

10. What simple descriptive name did Bernard Leach give to his manual for fellow craftsmen?

147

1. Which Italian nationalist founded Young Italy in the 1830s?

2. What was smuggled from Alexandria to Venice in, it is said, a barrel of pork?

3. Who landed in Sicily with a thousand Redshirts?

4. *Dafne*, performed in Florence in 1597, is the first known example of what new art form?

5. Who was appointed foreign minister by his father-in-law in the 1930s and sentenced to death by his father-in-law in the 1940s?

6. What new facility, leading to the development of the piano, was added to a harpsichord in the late seventeenth century?

7. Which Italian city was the first to have a printing press?

8. Who directed the film *Bicycle Thieves*, a classic of Italian neorealism?

9. Where and as what did Napoleon have himself crowned in 1805?

10. Which English poet died in Rome at the age of twenty-five?

148

1. What name is given to the symphony in which Haydn gave a subtle hint to his employer that it was time for the musicians to return to their homes?

2. Which Russian composer wrote a rhapsody on an Italian theme in his Swiss villa in the 1930s?

3. Of which joint work did William Walton and Edith Sitwell give a private performance in 1922?

4. Who was attacked in *Pravda* for providing 'chaos instead of music'?

5. Who composed, in the early 1970s, the first of his two concertos for sitar and orchestra?

6. Which of his operas was incomplete when Puccini died?

7. Which seven-year-old violinist gave his first professional performance playing Mendelssohn's *Violin Concerto* in San Francisco?

8. Which contralto made her London debut singing Handel's *Messiah* in Westminster Abbey during the Second World War?

9. Which Russian composer became greatly influenced by the theosophy of Madame Blavatsky?

10. Which German composer used three separate orchestras to achieve acoustic space in *Gruppen*?

149

1. Which campaigning league was formed in 1838 by seven Manchester merchants and mill-owners?

2. Vaughan Williams based his seventh symphony on the music he had written for a film – which film?

3. Which war began when Frederick the Great marched suddenly into Saxony?

4. Which US swimmer won seven gold medals at the Munich Olympics?

5. Who was elected by a permanent group of seven, consisting of four hereditary German princes and the archbishops of Mainz, Cologne and Trier?

6. Which group, expecting an imminent Second Coming, became an organized church in the USA in the 1860s?

7. The length of the new working week adopted in first-century Rome was based on which group of seven?

8. What was the name of Britain's first car for the popular market, launched by Herbert Austin in 1922?

9. Which film by Ingmar Bergman won the Jury Prize at Cannes in 1957?

10. What name did seven southern states, meeting in Montgomery, Alabama, choose for their dissident group?

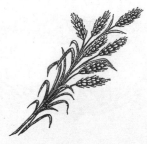

150

1. What name, in honour of the treasurer of the British Navy, did John Strong give to some remote islands he discovered in the Atlantic in the 1690s?

2. What Gypsy name did Augustus John give to his favourite subject, Dorothy McNeill?

3. What significant volume was published in London by John Heminge and Henry Condell?

4. Which much-loved poem was written by John McRae after a friend was killed in the First World War trenches?

5. What is the name of the TV show devised by John de Mol and first broadcast in the Netherlands in the 1990s?

6. What did John Hampden refuse to pay?

7. What did John Snow prove by studying the use of a pump in London's Broadwick Street?

8. Which 'cool jazz' group was formed by the pianist John Lewis?

9. For what was John Scopes prosecuted in Tennessee in the 1920s?

10. In which African country did Johnny Koroma mount a briefly successful military coup in the 1990s?

151

1. What name was used for the system that Napoleon imposed on continental Europe in the early nineteenth century, designed to strangle Britain's trade?

2. In which Netherlands town did members of the European Union sign a treaty preparing for the introduction of the euro?

3. Who wrote *The Economic Consequences of the Peace* in response to the terms imposed by the Allies at Versailles?

4. What two words followed *The Economic Consequences of* ... in the title of a book by British economist Nicholas Kaldor attacking monetarism?

5. In which Italian city were the Bardi and Peruzzi families bankrupted when the English king, Edward III, defaulted on his massive debts?

6. Where in New Hampshire were the World Bank and the IMF conceived, towards the end of the Second World War?

7. What title did Ernst Friedrich Schumacher give to the book of the 1970s in which he foresaw the need to safeguard the world's scarce resources?

8. What phrase did first-time presidential candidate F. D. Roosevelt use when pledging to deliver to the American people new economic policies?

9. In which Ionian city in western Turkey were the first coins minted, in the seventh century BC?

10. Where in New York was an informal financial market transformed to become the New York Stock and Exchange Board?

152

1. Which athlete won four gold medals in the 1984 Los Angeles Olympics?

2. Why did Adolf Hitler choose a particular railway carriage for the signing of the armistice that signalled the defeat of France in 1940?

3. Which people's relentless advance into Europe was halted by defeat somewhere between Poitiers and Tours?

4. Whom did Gary Kasparov defeat to become the youngest ever world champion?

5. Which lethal weapon helped the Swiss to defeat the Habsburg Army at Morgarten in 1315?

6. Which people won a victory at Kosovo in 1389?

7. Where was a British army virtually annihilated by Zulu tribesmen in 1879?

8. Which leader of a junta resigned three days after his country lost the war that he had instigated in 1982?

9. Who led the Pakistan cricket team to victory in the World Cup of 1992?

10. Who defeated the veteran Ken Rosewall in the finals of his first Wimbledon and US Open titles, both in 1974?

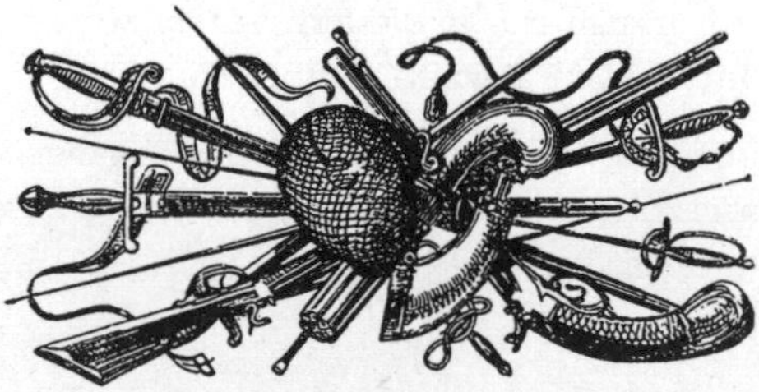

153

1. Who discovered the first law of electrolysis, and then followed it a year later with the second law?

2. Whose album *Thriller* sold 40 million copies within ten years?

3. On whose novel was Anthony Minghella's film *The English Patient* based?

4. Who established a new style of literary biography with his two-volume life of Lytton Strachey?

5. Which Flemish-born sculptor created the monument to Newton in Westminster Abbey?

6. Whom did David Cameron succeed as leader of the Conservative Party in Britain?

7. Which English potter set up a studio in the 1920s at Winchcombe, in Gloucestershire?

8. Whose play *Copenhagen* dramatized the visit of Werner Heisenberg to Niels Bohr in wartime Denmark?

9. Who made his name starring in *Alfie* and *The Ipcress File* in the same year?

10. Who wrote the oratorio *A Child of Our Time*?

154

1. Who was Queen Victoria's favourite painter of animals, whom she honoured with a knighthood?

2. Who, in a paper on the 'psychology and psychopathology of animals', announced his discovery of the conditioned reflex?

3. What new service cut to ten days the delivery time of mail going from Missouri to California?

4. By what nickname is the John Updike character Harry Angstrom known?

5. In which part of the world was Phar Lap famous and popular in the 1930s?

6. What codename was used by the Germans for Hitler's planned invasion of England?

7. Which famous painted Buddhist caves in India were accidentally discovered by British officers more interested in shooting tigers?

8. Which French scientist wrote the seminal text *Research on the Fossil Bones of Quadrupeds*?

9. Which kind of animal features in the title of the first volume of Cormac McCarthy's trilogy set in Mexico?

10. Which plane, designed by De Havilland, was used to train nearly all British pilots during the Second World War?

155

1. Which US author wrote *The Autocrat of the Breakfast Table*, which became the first of a breakfast-table series?

2. Who won control in Ravenna by inviting Odoacer to a banquet and murdering him during the meal?

3. What title did William Burroughs give to his account of the horrors of a junkie's life?

4. Who organized a famous series of lunchtime concerts during the Second World War in London's National Gallery?

5. What is the name of the Christian sacrament established during the Last Supper?

6. Who painted a celebration of the Stuart dynasty on the ceiling of the Banqueting House in Whitehall?

7. Which Japanese ceremony, developed in the thirteenth and fourteenth centuries, was accompanied by exquisite wares from Japanese potters?

8. Who is the bewitching central character in Truman Capote's *Breakfast at Tiffany's*?

9. Who died in Babylon, following a banquet, eleven years after setting off from home?

10. Which US presidential candidate won on a platform promising 'the full dinner pail'?

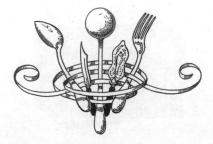

156

1. Which group of people migrated southwards, in the twelfth century, from a place they called Aztlan?

2. In which city did a Jewish community first use the word 'diaspora', in the third century BC?

3. Which was the most famous of the trails established in North America's Great Migration?

4. What name, derived from a biblical character, has been given to the tribes that migrated north from the Arabian peninsula into Palestine and Syria?

5. Which area provided the largest group of immigrants to the USA in the 1840s?

6. What collective name has been given to the Indo-European tribes that moved into India from the north-west about 3500 years ago?

7. Which ship brought the first group of West Indian immigrants to Britain after the Second World War?

8. Which group of people gave their name to Palestine, where they settled about 3200 years ago?

9. Into which area was a German tribe, the Cimbri, moving until they were defeated at Vercellae?

10. What was the tribal origin of the group which settled in France as Normans in the early tenth century?

157

1. By what name was William Joyce known in Britain during the Second World War?

2. Why did a radical political club in Paris become known as the Jacobins?

3. By what name did Zoroastrians, fleeing from Iran, become known after arriving in India?

4. Which Flemish painter, a contemporary of Jan van Eyck, is also known as the Master of Flémalle?

5. By what name did Kingsley Amis and other young British writers become known in the 1950s?

6. By what name is the sixteenth-century event known in which eighty distinguished Swedish citizens were executed together in the capital city's main square?

7. By what joint name were Germany and Italy known after Hitler and Mussolini formed an alliance?

8. Who is traditionally said to have designed a device, now known by his name, to enable the king of Syracuse to raise water from the holds of his ships?

9. The followers of John Wycliffe became known after his death by what name, meaning 'mutterers'?

10. What names were given to the two profoundly influential type faces developed in Venice in the late fifteenth century?

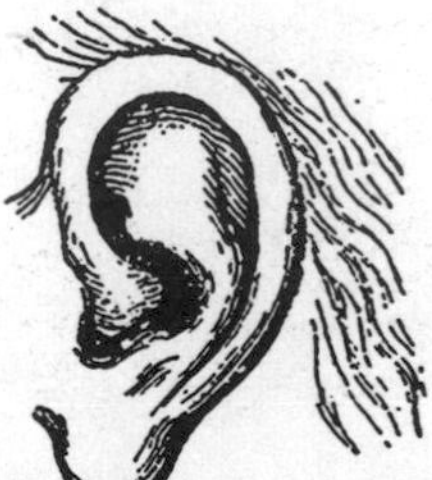

158

1. Massive stone heads were a characteristic part of the artistic tradition of which Central American people?

2. Who had a two-ounce stone cut from his bladder in 1658?

3. In which city did a newspaper proprietor give Henry Morton Stanley a concise commission: 'Find Livingstone'?

4. Who deciphered Egyptian hieroglyphs with the help of the inscriptions on the Rosetta Stone?

5. At which club, in London's Oxford Street, did the Rolling Stones first perform as a group?

6. Which Russian poet's first collection, published in 1913, was called *Stone*?

7. A stone in Scotland dating from 1511 is the earliest-known example of its kind – what kind?

8. Which powerful anti-war film was made in 1930 by Lewis Milestone, from a German novel published the previous year?

9. Which pope laid the foundation stone for the present St Peter's in Rome?

10. Which ancient village in the Orkneys has built-in furniture made of stone?

159

1. Who is the 'man of property' in the title of the first in the series of novels in which he features?

2. Whose novel *Swami and Friends* was the first to be set in his fictional town of Malgudi?

3. Which New Zealand author's first collection of stories was called *In a German Pension*?

4. What was the title of the Edgar Rice Burroughs novel in which Tarzan first featured?

5. Of what very fashionable literary trend was one of the first examples *A Universal History of Infamy* by Jorge Luis Borges?

6. Which character, created by Joel Chandler Harris, made his first appearance in the 1870s?

7. Which novel by Aphra Behn was one of the first published polemics against the inhumanity of the African slave trade?

8. Radclyffe Hall's 1928 novel *The Well of Loneliness* was a literary breakthrough in what sense?

9. Which secret agent thrilled his readers for the first time in John Buchan's novel *The Thirty-Nine Steps*?

10. Which Canadian author published her first novel, *The Edible Woman*, in 1969?

160

1. Who designed a succession of four chronometers in the eighteenth century, in pursuit of a prize?

2. By what name did four Scottish painters become known after exhibiting together in Paris?

3. For what is the Iffley Road track particularly famous?

4. Who extended a boastful account of his own sexual adventures to four notoriously explicit volumes, published in the 1920s as *My Life and Loves*?

5. Whose last work was sung by Kirsten Flagstad at a London premiere after the composer's death?

6. Which was Alain-Fournier's first and only novel?

7. Who set out Four Noble Truths and the Eightfold Path in his first sermon?

8. What were Henry Morton Stanley's immortal four words?

9. Who sculpted the four massive presidential portraits at Mount Rushmore?

10. Who won the first of four Oscars with her second film, *Morning Glory*?

161

1. What new name did the tsar Nicholas II give to his capital city, for political reasons, in 1914?

2. In which early piece by Arnold Schoenberg does a solo voice recite the text to the accompaniment of a quintet?

3. In what context did Karl Peters achieve rapid results for Otto von Bismarck in the 1880s?

4. What description of Peter Pan forms the subtitle of J. M. Barrie's play?

5. What significant purchase did Peter Minuit make in the 1620s?

6. Which Austrian dramatist gave his first play the provocative title *Offending the Audience*?

7. In what context did Peter the Hermit, an old monk on a donkey, become famous at the end of the eleventh century?

8. Who directed the trilogy of films based on *The Lord of the Rings*?

9. Who designed the cover for the Beatles album *Sergeant Pepper's Lonely Hearts Club Band*?

10. Which leader of Vichy France was sentenced at the end of the war as a collaborator and executed?

162

1. Which group of people were expelled from Spain in the 1490s?

2. Which composer wrote a series of twelve piano pieces with the title *Iberia*?

3. What shorter name is used for Rodrigo Díaz, who captured Valencia from the Muslims in the late eleventh century?

4. Which golfer became no. 1 in Europe in 1976, before his twentieth birthday?

5. Which soldier, recovering in 1521 from a serious wound, read the lives of the saints and was inspired to devote his own life to Jesus?

6. Which director satirized social conventions in his film *The Discreet Charm of the Bourgeoisie*?

7. Whose marriage brought together the crowns of Aragon and Castile, creating a virtually unified Spain?

8. Which poet and playwright was arrested and shot by Falange militia in the first month of the Spanish Civil War?

9. Which fifteen-year-old guitarist gave his first public performance in Granada in 1909?

10. Who, in the 1650s, did a large painting of himself painting the king and queen of Spain?

163

1. Which prestigious British steeplechase dates only from 1924?

2. In which 1981 film did Henry and Jane Fonda star with Katharine Hepburn?

3. Which opera, the first in a sequence of four, had its premiere in Munich in 1869?

4. In what ship did Francis Drake make his three-year round-the-world voyage?

5. Who was the unsuccessful Republican candidate when Lyndon B. Johnson was elected president?

6. Which Israeli prime minister resigned in the 1970s and was succeeded by Yitzhak Rabin?

7. From which sacred building did Indira Gandhi use troops to expel militant Sikhs?

8. What is the title of James Frazer's great compilation of ritual and religious custom?

9. Which eighteenth-century Italian dramatist made very effective use of the *commedia dell'arte* tradition?

10. Which eleven-year-old Austrian composer had a huge success in Vienna in 1910 with a pantomime opera, *The Snowman*?

164

1. The king of which country was killed by an anarchist, Gaetano Bresci, in the first months of the twentieth century?

2. Which US president was visiting the Pan-American Exposition in Buffalo, New York, when he was assassinated in 1901?

3. Which prime minister of Burma was assassinated by political rivals during a meeting in 1947?

4. Who was assassinated by Nathuram Godse at a prayer meeting in 1948?

5. In which country was the young king Faisal II murdered in a coup led by Abdul Karim Qassim?

6. Which prime minister was stabbed to death in the South African parliament in 1966?

7. Who was assassinated by Sirhan Sirhan in a Los Angeles hotel?

8. Whom did Muslim terrorists assassinate in Egypt in 1981?

9. Which president of the Democratic Republic of the Congo was assassinated in 2001 during an attempted coup?

10. Which controversial Dutch politician was assassinated outside a radio station in Hilversum in 2002?

165

1. Who established themselves in Hungary in the ninth century, under the leadership of Arpad?

2. Exceptional remains of which people have been found in frozen burial mounds at Pazyryk, in Siberia?

3. Which people were in control of Spain when the Muslims arrived from Africa in the eighth century?

4. Which group of people inhabited Chichén Itzá, which was excavated by Edward Herbert Thompson?

5. Which group, led by Gaiseric, made Carthage their base for Mediterranean raids in the fifth century?

6. The southern part of which continent was largely inhabited, from about 2000 BC, by the Khoisan?

7. Which people, known now by one aspect of their ceramics, arrived in Britain about 4000 years ago?

8. Which modern state of the USA was the territory of the Pueblo Indians, who rose against the Spanish colonists in 1680?

9. Of which tribes was Temujin elected chief early in the thirteenth century, taking the name by which he is now known?

10. Which Turks ruled from Baghdad from the second half of the eleventh century?

166

1. Under what nickname did the British entrepreneur George Hudson acquire seemingly royal status in the 1840s?

2. What was the surname of the brothers George and Ira, who together wrote twenty-two musicals in seventeen years?

3. Which French artist crossed the Atlantic to sculpt George Washington from life at Mount Vernon?

4. Britain's George Cross was created to reward heroism by members of which group of people?

5. What name did the German chemist Georg Stahl give to the substance which he believed to be released in the process of burning?

6. Which author created George Folanshee Babbitt, a real-estate broker in the midwestern town of Zenith?

7. In which city did the British East India Company construct Fort St George?

8. What was the title of George du Maurier's most successful novel, published in the 1890s?

9. Which outlaw lived secretly for a year in the Wartburg castle, near Eisenach, and was known to the locals as Junker Georg?

10. In honour of whom did George Gilbert Scott design a great memorial shrine in the 1860s?

167

1. Which new version of a very old kind of weapon gave the English victory over the Scots at Falkirk in 1298?

2. What insect-like name did the British public use from 1944 for the German *Vergeltungswaffe 1*?

3. At which test site in the New Mexican desert did US scientists explode the first atom bomb?

4. What firing mechanism for a musket was introduced in the early seventeenth century and remained standard until the nineteenth century?

5. Which British author used the title *Sword of Honour* for his trilogy of Second World War novels?

6. Who starred in a silent film called simply *It*, thus acquiring her famous nickname, the 'It girl'?

7. Which American Imagist poet published a collection called *Sword Blades and Poppy Seed*?

8. What powerful but portable weapon did the Chinese develop in the third century BC, many centuries before its first use in Europe?

9. Which British group launched an influential new style of music in 1975 with their first gig, at St Martin's School of Art in London?

10. What new kind of siege engine did the Macedonians develop for the armies of Philip II and Alexander the Great?

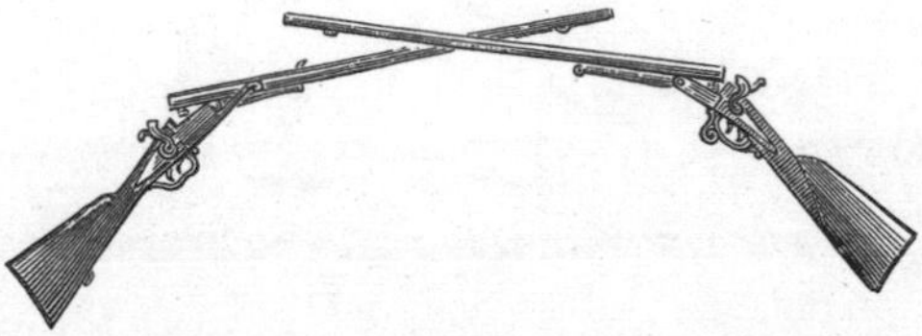

168

1. Who was champion jockey in Britain twenty-six times, beginning in 1925?

2. Which Formula One driver appeared on the podium in every one of his first seven races, on the two last occasions as winner?

3. In which sport did Maurice ‘Rocket’ Richard become the first to score fifty goals in a single season?

4. Who became the first player to achieve tennis’s Grand Slam for a second time, in 1969?

5. The last game that Stanley Matthews played for his home-town football club was thirty-three years after his first professional appearance with them. Which club?

6. Which twenty-year-old knocked out Trevor Berbick in the 1980s to become the youngest ever world heavyweight champion?

7. Which English athlete set an Olympic and world record in the decathlon at the 1984 Los Angeles Olympics?

8. Who became, in the 1950s, the first football player to win 100 caps for England?

9. Which English jockey won the Derby a record nine times?

10. In what sport was the First World Series played between nine leading teams in 1903?

169

1. What name is given to the eleven ships that left Porstmouth for Australia in 1787?

2. Who was captain of the English cricket team during the 'bodyline' controversy?

3. Which gang were the subject of Australia's first feature-length film?

4. Which nineteen-year-old won the women's singles title at Wimbledon for the first time in 1971?

5. What began with a discovery at Ballarat, followed by another a few months later at Bendigo?

6. Which Aboriginal sprinter lit the cauldron to launch the Sydney Olympic Games in 2000?

7. Which author wrote *Australia Felix*, the first of three novels about her father?

8. Who was the first Australian to win the Nobel Prize for Literature?

9. Which fictional housewife made her first appearance in a Melbourne revue, before becoming much more widely known?

10. To the nearest round number, what was Donald Bradman's career average as a batsman when he retired from Test cricket?

170

1. In which play by Pierre Beaumarchais did Figaro make his first appearance?

2. On which English actor of the old school did Ronald Harwood partly base his play *The Dresser*?

3. Which dramatist had his first great success with the tragedy *Andromaque* in 1667?

4. Which company was set up by Bertolt Brecht in Berlin in the late 1940s?

5. Where in Bavaria did a lasting tradition begin when a Passion play was first performed there in the 1630s?

6. Who first performed John Osborne's character Archie Rice?

7. The name of which sixth-century Greek performer has been traditionally applied to the entire profession?

8. In which entirely appropriate setting did T. S. Eliot's play *Murder in the Cathedral* have its first performance?

9. Which play of Arthur Miller's was a metaphor for the contemporary paranoia of the McCarthy witch hunt for Communists?

10. On which musical did Leonard Bernstein, Jerome Robbins and Stephen Sondheim collaborate in the late 1950s?

171

1. By what name is Tchaikovsky's symphony no. 6 known?

2. Which region was brutally ruled in the seventeenth century by a tribunal known as the Council of Blood?

3. By what name did the Dutch artist Gerrit Dou and his followers become known, because of the exquisite precision of their work?

4. What name was later given to the extraordinary form of three-dimensional image first created by Dennis Gabor?

5. In which island did an armed uprising against Spanish rule, known as the 'Grito de Lares', take place?

6. What did the philosophy taught by Plotinus in Rome become known as, identifying it as a development of an earlier tradition?

7. A simpler version of Egyptian hieroglyphs, developed for use by ordinary people, became known by what Greek name?

8. By what name did St Jerome's Latin translation of the Bible later become known?

9. The elite troops of the ancient Persian empire were known by what flattering name?

10. Cleopatra's son, born in Rome, became known as what because of his probable paternity?

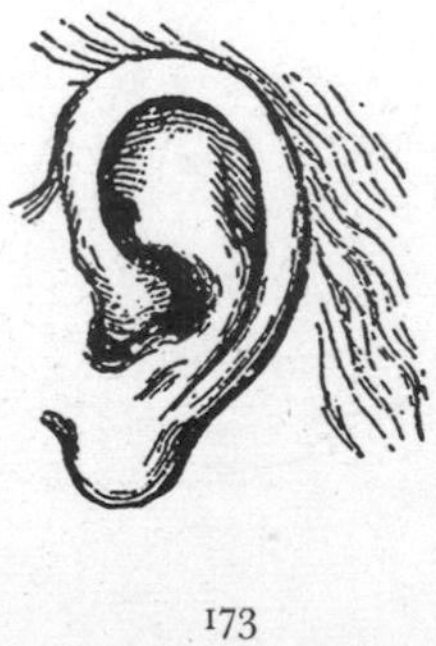

172

1. Which ancient Irish game acquired formal status in the 1870s?

2. What name was taken by the twenty-six counties of southern Ireland when they became a separate nation?

3. What secret Protestant group was formed in County Armagh in the late eighteenth century?

4. Which Irish republican was the first woman to be elected to Britain's House of Commons but refused to take her seat?

5. Which venerable king of Munster defeated the Vikings at Clontarf but was killed in his tent after the battle?

6. Which dance, based on traditional Irish step dancing, became popular from the mid 1990s?

7. In which royalist stronghold did Oliver Cromwell authorize the massacre of some 2800 people?

8. What unprecedented step was taken by Terence O'Neill and Sean Lemass?

9. Which organization, to campaign for an independent Ireland, was launched by Arthur Griffith early in the twentieth century?

10. What dramatic event was the start of the Easter Rising?

173

1. Which two brothers formed a Holy Club at Oxford?

2. Which early governor of Massachusetts wrote a journal later published as *The History of New England*?

3. Which is now the best known of the poems in John Masefield's collection of *Salt-Water Ballads*?

4. A Liverpool group of musicians first called themselves Long John & . . . what?

5. Who played Tarzan in *Tarzan the Ape Man*, the first of countless Tarzan talkies?

6. Who set off with two ships, *Erebus* and *Terror*, to search for the Northwest Passage?

7. Which US economist criticized modern consumerism in *The Affluent Society*?

8. Which prime minister of Australia was dismissed by the governor-general, Sir John Kerr?

9. The first example of what annual item was designed in the 1840s by John Calcott Horsley for Henry Cole?

10. What modern device did John Harrington describe and illustrate in his pamphlet *The Metamorphosis of Ajax*?

174

1. What gas, much in the news nowadays, was identified by Joseph Black in the 1750s?

2. Who made a safer explosive by combining the volatile nitroglycerine with kieselguhr?

3. What colour was the first synthetic dye, accidentally created by the English chemist William Henry Perkin?

4. Which drug caused severe abnormalities in about 12,000 children during the late 1950s?

5. The nuclei of which two elements formed in the first three minutes after Big Bang?

6. What new method of scientific dating was developed by Willard Libby?

7. Of what does the first known description appear in a Chinese manual on warfare in the eleventh century?

8. What word, meaning 'same place' in Greek, was coined by Frederick Soddy?

9. When the Dutch chemist Jan Baptist van Helmont suggested that there might be insubstantial substances other than air, what word did he invent for such a substance?

10. What new facility, with dramatic social repercussions, was developed by a small chemical company in Mexico City in the early 1950s?

175

1. Who invented the Frankenstein phenomenon, with her Gothic novel about life given to an artificial man?

2. Which British designer launched the miniskirt?

3. Which twelve-year-old Dorset girl discovered the 6.4-metre fossil of an icthyosaur at Lyme Regis?

4. Which US state derives from the territory granted by Charles I as a haven for English Roman Catholics?

5. Which Jamaican-born nurse set up her own hospital to nurse wounded British soldiers in the Crimea?

6. Who expounded her beliefs in *Science and Health with Key to the Scriptures*?

7. Which cricket club ended a long-running controversy by declaring that overarm bowling was legitimate?

8. Which Englishwoman, in Turkey in 1717, submitted her son to the local system of inoculation against smallpox?

9. Which St Petersburg company was the first in which Vaslav Nijinsky and his sister Bronislava danced?

10. Who drowned in a tragic accident at Chappaquiddick in the 1960s?

176

1. Who went to work as a missionary at Lambarene, in west Africa?

2. In which religion are the Upanishads early mystic texts?

3. *A Tale of the Christ* was the subtitle of which novel by Lew Wallace?

4. The building of which holy city was begun by Arjan, the fifth Sikh guru?

5. Which clergyman created Uncle Toby and the Widow Wadman?

6. Which religion was spread through much of India by the enthusiastic support of the emperor Asoka?

7. Which so-called city became an exceptionally small nation-state through the Lateran Treaty?

8. During which dynasty was the Temple of Heaven built in Beijing?

9. What did Pope Innocent III outlaw, as a weapon of mass destruction?

10. Who was the first black archbishop of Cape Town?

177

1. Which seaside resort in Texas was demolished by a hurricane in 1900?

2. What was the USA the first nation to do on a regular basis, beginning in 1790?

3. By what name is the revival movement known that was led by Jonathan Edwards in the 1730s?

4. Which novelist killed himself with a shotgun in his log cabin in Idaho?

5. What term was coined to describe President Dwight Eisenhower's view of how states might fall to Communism?

6. Which US city was largely destroyed by fire in 1871, providing the opportunity for a very successful period of reconstruction?

7. Which Indian tribe were the victims in a massacre by US troops at Wounded Knee Creek, South Dakota?

8. To whom was the Olive Branch Petition of 1775 personally addressed?

9. What name did Thomas Jefferson choose for the mansion he began constructing in Virginia in 1770?

10. What was the intended destination of Meriwether Lewis and William Clark when they left St Louis in 1804?

178

1. The battle between the *Monitor* and the *Merrimack* was the first clash between what kind of ships?

2. By which enemy were the British warships *Prince of Wales* and *Repulse* destroyed?

3. Who worked as a ship's carpenter in Dutch and English shipyards in the late seventeenth century, even though he didn't need the job?

4. What was the immediate purpose of the fleet sent by Darius I across the Aegean early in the fifth century BC?

5. Into which crowded harbour did Francis Drake sail and destroy some thirty Spanish ships?

6. Who commanded the powerful US fleet that finally persuaded the Japanese to open their country to western trade in 1854?

7. Which religious leader was captured in St Andrews in the mid sixteenth century and was sent to serve in the French fleet as a galley slave?

8. What name was given to the ships made in the USA as part of Lend-Lease support to the Allies in the Second World War?

9. In which short Disney animated film did Mickey Mouse make his first appearance?

10. In which harbour did French crews scuttle their fleet to prevent it falling into German hands?

179

1. Which German field marshal disobeyed Hitler and surrendered at Stalingrad?

2. Who expounded his theory of existentialism in *Being and Nothingness*?

3. Which composer set Rainer Maria Rilke's song cycle *Das Marienleben*?

4. What was the destination that Paul Revere never reached, on his famous and urgent ride?

5. Which British theoretical physicist predicted the existence of an anti-particle discovered two years later and named the positron?

6. Under what name and number did Giovanni Montini become better known?

7. Which schoolfriend of Bill Gates was his partner in the founding of Microsoft?

8. Who was the last visitor received by Jean-Paul Marat?

9. Who played the lead in the first production of Robert Bolt's play *A Man for All Seasons*?

10. Which prime minister of the Transvaal formed an alliance with the other Boer republic, the Orange Free State, in the 1890s?

180

1. What insect did geneticist Thomas Hunt Morgan use in his experiments to establish the chromosome theory of heredity?

2. Which was the first of Richard Wagner's major operas to be staged?

3. What dismissive treatment of the French consul by the Turkish governor of Algiers led indirectly to a French blockade and then invasion?

4. What was the title of Jean-Paul Sartre's first play?

5. In which film did Fred Astaire and Ginger Rogers dance together for the first time?

6. What name is given to the sudden departure from Ireland in 1607 of the leaders of the powerful Tyrone and Tyrconnel families?

7. In which chilling novel is the fat boy Piggy the victim?

8. What is the title of the twelve short piano pieces that became Robert Schumann's first published composition?

9. What is the modern name for the Aerial Medical Service?

10. What invention by John Kay made a major contribution to the Lancashire woollen industry?

181

1. What feat was an Irish packet steamer, the *Sirius*, the first to achieve in 1838?

2. Which was the world's first commercial jet airliner, launched in the 1940s?

3. What great project was completed with a meeting at Promontory Summit in 1869?

4. Which Scottish engineer provided an improved surface for a road near Bristol in the 1810s?

5. The first prototype of what machine crossed the English Channel in the 1950s?

6. For what event did thousands of distinguished guests gather at Port Said in the 1860s?

7. Which was the first major Roman road, linking Rome with Capua and completed in the late fourth century BC?

8. Which two seas were linked for shipping by the Göta Canal, completed in the 1830s?

9. Which model, launched in 1959, became the best-selling British car of all time?

10. Of what was London's Metropolitan Railway the first example in the world?

182

1. Which two political terms of abuse emerged in England in the early 1640s?

2. What rich new English tradition did Handel launch, with *Esther* as the first example?

3. What veto by George III caused William Pitt to resign at the start of the nineteenth century?

4. Of which card game did Edmond Hoyle publish in 1742 a definitive set of rules?

5. Who, in his *Principles*, defined 'utility' as that which enhances pleasure and reduces pain?

6. Who held her nerve in the Bedchamber Crisis?

7. What new name for their enterprise was adopted in the 1770s by the London brokers who met to do business in Jonathan's Coffee House?

8. Some of the future Pilgrim Fathers had made a previous sea voyage twelve years earlier – from Lincolnshire to which country?

9. Who was celebrated by Edmund Spenser as a 'faerie queene'?

10. The first English chartered company, licensed by Mary I, was granted a monopoly to trade with which area?

183

1. Who, in exile on the island of Rathlin, was supposedly taught a lesson by a single-minded arachnid?

2. Which composer threw himself into the Rhine, in an attempt to commit suicide, and spent the last two years of his life in an asylum?

3. Which Scottish painter published lithographs from his travels in *The Holy Land, Syria, Idumea, Arabia, Egypt & Nubia*?

4. Who was prime minister when a Conservative administration reintroduced income tax in Britain, in the 1840s, at a level of about 3 per cent?

5. Who said *Goodbye to All That* in his autobiography?

6. Whose uprising ended in disaster, in the early nineteenth century, when he marched on Dublin with only about 100 men?

7. Who choreographed the ballet scenes danced by Moira Shearer in the film *The Red Shoes*?

8. Who is seen skating on Duddingston Loch in a painting attributed to Henry Raeburn?

9. Which architect returned to Britain in the 1750s with a repertoire of classical themes, after two years in Rome?

10. Who first observed the inverse proportion between pressure and volume in any gas?

184

1. The Roman emperor Aurelian, setting up a cult of the Unconquered Sun, decided that which day in December was the sun's birthday?

2. Who played the Sundance Kid?

3. When several smaller groups merged to form the Guomindang, or Nationalist Party, who became its leader?

4. Which street became famous after the Nestor Film Company opened Hollywood's first film studio there?

5. What startling conclusion about the solar system was reached by an ancient Greek astronomer in Samos?

6. Which seventeenth-century astronomer, working in Paris, was only 7 per cent out when he calculated the distance from the earth to the sun?

7. For what was Sun Myung Moon convicted and imprisoned in the USA?

8. In which city was there a Bloody Sunday when troops fired on demonstrators in 1905?

9. In which city was there a Bloody Sunday involving British security forces in 1920?

10. In which city did thirteen die on a Bloody Sunday in 1972?

185

1. In which state of the USA was the 75,000-barrel-a-day Lucas Gusher discovered early in the twentieth century?

2. What is the abbreviated title commonly used for Adam Smith's great work analysing the whole system of political economy?

3. What commodity brought great prosperity in the early twentieth century to the town of Manaus, thousands of miles up the Amazon?

4. What name was given to a belt along the border of Northern Rhodesia and the Belgian Congo because of the mineral discoveries there?

5. The name of the king who built the temple of Diana at Ephesus became a byword for extreme wealth – what name?

6. What is the title of Thorstein Veblen's late-nineteenth-century attack on the growth of capitalist 'consumerism'?

7. What website, put online less than two years previously, did Google buy for $1.65 billion?

8. What was found in the early twentieth century on property in South Africa belonging to Thomas Cullinan?

9. Who argued in his book *The Gospel of Wealth* that 'the man who dies rich dies disgraced'?

10. Which Scottish artist's massive bronze sculpture entitled *The Wealth of Nations* is in South Kyle, a district of Edinburgh?

186

1. By what name is the second phase of cubism known, characterized among other things by the use of collage?

2. Who moved from where to where in the event that became known as the Hegira?

3. By what name did the world heavyweight fight in Zaire between Muhammad Ali and George Foreman become known?

4. What was the real name of the man better known as El Greco?

5. By what name did Batu Khan and his Mongols become known after they settled in Russia?

6. By what name is the incident known which began in a church service in Italy and led to the massacre of 2000 French residents?

7. What nickname was applied to Jean-Claude Duvalier, reflecting the related name given to his father?

8. What did the alliance between Octavian, Mark Antony and Lepidus become known as?

9. The entire land surface of the earth merged at one point into a single continent, known now by what name?

10. In what type of activity was the group nicknamed the Britpack involved?

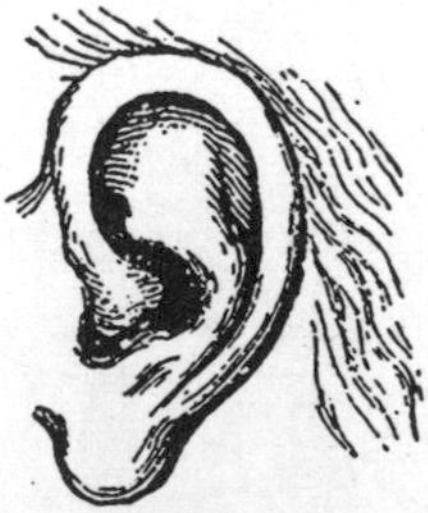

187

1. In which colony was the Young Kikuyu Association formed to fight for African rights?

2. Which partial individual, living about 3 million years ago, was named from a Beatles song?

3. For what trade was a new town, Zawila, established in the Sahara in about AD 700?

4. Who brought South Africa into the Second World War on becoming prime minister?

5. What name, with a modern resonance, is given to the Shona kingdom that became dominant in the thirteenth century?

6. Which playwright and pro-democracy campaigner was hanged by the junta ruling Nigeria?

7. What town was built outside Johannesburg to house the city's black labour force?

8. Who declared Katanga to be an independent state?

9. Which hereditary ruler was banned by the British government from returning to Bechuanaland?

10. Whom did Winston Churchill appoint to command the 8th Army in north Africa in August 1942?

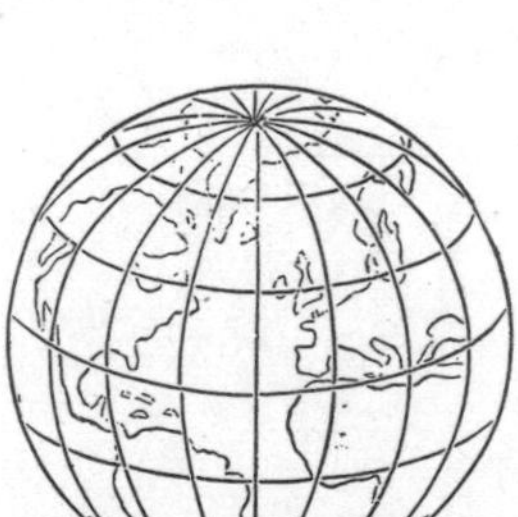

188

1. Who, in the first century, destroyed her enemies' headquarters at Colchester?

2. Which place in the Arabian peninsula was a favourite place of pilgrimage in the second century, with a famous collection of idols?

3. What Roman items, surviving from the third century in dry Egyptian tombs, are the earliest known examples of knitting?

4. The definitive contents of what holy text were at last established, in the fourth century, in a document distributed by the bishop of Alexandria?

5. Who murdered his brother, Bleda, in the fifth century, to become the sole ruler of the Huns?

6. Which city was founded by people seeking refuge on islands in a lagoon to escape from hordes of invading Lombards in the sixth century?

7. From which supernatural being did Muhammad hear the message that he began preaching in Mecca in the seventh century?

8. In which country did an empress in the eighth century commission the first known (and very large-scale) printing project?

9. Which invaders captured Dublin in the ninth century and established a kingdom there?

10. Where did Eric Thorvaldsson sail to in the tenth century, when he was exiled for three years from Iceland?

189

1. On which Atlantic island did the parliament, the *althing*, pass in about 1000 a resolution that everyone on the island was to be baptized?

2. Which son of William the Conqueror became king of England in 1100?

3. What is the name, meaning 'pure ones', of the heretical Christians who by 1200 even had bishops of their own in the south of France?

4. The year 1300 was proclaimed as the first in what ongoing series in the Roman Catholic church?

5. What name was adopted in Germany by the guilds of singers and songwriters that were developing in around 1400?

6. Where did the Portuguese explorer Pedro Cabral, with a fleet of thirteen ships, make landfall in 1500 with far-reaching consequences?

7. Of what musical form is a work by Emilio de' Cavalieri considered the first example, performed in 1600 in the Oratory in Rome?

8. Charles II of Spain, dying childless in 1700, surprised and alarmed Europe by leaving all his territories to a young prince of which nation?

9. Where, after leading his army through snow-filled Alpine passes, did Napoleon defeat an Austrian army in 1800?

10. Which oratorio by Elgar, setting Cardinal Newman's poem of the same title, was first performed in 1900?

190

1. For a new brand, launched in 1900, Daimler used the name of the daughter of one of their investors – what name?

2. Thomas Mann published in 1901 his first novel, a saga about a bourgeois family in decline. What is its title?

3. What drink did a North Carolina pharmacist, Caleb Bradham, begin to market in 1902 from the back room of his shop?

4. Irish author Erskine Childers had a bestseller in 1903 with a thriller about a planned German invasion of Britain. What was it called?

5. Who, although entirely blind and deaf, graduated *cum laude* from Radcliffe College in 1904?

6. On which battleship was there a complaint in 1905 about maggoty meat, leading to violent repercussions?

7. What word did the English biologist William Bateson use in 1906 to describe the phenomenon of heredity and variation?

8. Which third nation formed in 1907 a Triple Entente with Britain and France?

9. Which great Russian bass did Sergei Diaghilev present in *Boris Godunov* at the Paris Opéra in 1908?

10. What did the French biologist Charles Nicolle discover in 1909 to be the villain in spreading epidemic typhus?

191

1. Who conducted, in Munich in 1910, the first performance of an eighth symphony subsequently known as the *Symphony of a Thousand*?

2. Which chancellor of the exchequer introduced national insurance in Britain in 1911?

3. Who moved to Cambridge in 1912 specifically to study philosophy under Bertrand Russell?

4. In which region did a Volunteer Force of 100,000 men begin drilling with dummy wooden rifles in 1913?

5. What was the name of the movement launched by Wyndham Lewis and others in 1914 with a new magazine called *Blast*?

6. What new range of heat-resistant kitchenware was launched in the USA in 1915 by the Corning Glass Company?

7. What name did Karl Liebknecht and Rosa Luxemburg choose for their radical political movement, founded in Germany in 1916?

8. What system, introduced by the Allies in 1917, reduced at last the number of ships lost to German U-boats in the Atlantic?

9. Along what river in France did the Allies halt a German advance in 1918 and begin a successful counterattack with tanks?

10. In which famous room in France was the peace treaty between the Allies and Germany signed in 1919?

192

1. Which Bristol-born actor, subsequently a major film star, moved to the USA in 1920 with a troupe of touring tumblers?

2. What was the R-38, which met with disaster in 1921?

3. Which novel was published in 1922 by Sylvia Beach in Paris, because of censorship problems elsewhere?

4. Which region did France forcibly occupy, with Belgian support, in 1923?

5. Which group of four brothers made their Broadway debut in 1924?

6. Which civilian encryption machine did the Germans adapt for military purposes in 1925?

7. Which book, published in 1926, described its author's role in the Arab uprising during the First World War?

8. Which Staffordshire potter launched in 1927 the highly coloured ceramics that she called her Bizarre Ware?

9. Which English sculptor received in 1928 his first commission, from London Underground?

10. Which comic-strip character made his first appearance in 1929, in the land of the Soviets?

193

1. In what field did the Hays Code set exacting standards in the USA from 1930?

2. What new paramilitary group was set up in 1931 in Palestine by Zionists impatient with the policies of the Haganah?

3. Who was able to form an administration after the partial victory of Fianna Fáil in the election of 1932?

4. Which Austrian chancellor suspended parliament in 1933 and outlawed the Nazi Party?

5. Who glorified Hitler and the Nuremberg rally in 1934 in *Triumph of the Will*?

6. When Alban Berg died, in 1935, which of his operas was incomplete?

7. Who caused a stir in 1936 by attending the opening of an exhibition in a diving suit?

8. Hans Krebs discovered in 1937 something often now referred to by his name – what?

9. In which novel of 1938 did Evelyn Waugh introduce Lord Copper, proprietor of *The Beast*?

10. What was the full title of the British radio programme, launched in 1939, for which *ITMA* became the standard abbreviation?

194

1. What, according to Neville Chamberlain, had Hitler missed by the spring of 1940?

2. From which island did German forces evict the British in 1941, after a week-long battle?

3. Who was appointed president of German-occupied Norway in 1942?

4. What garments were favoured by Mexican American youths and were associated with riots involving them in 1943?

5. Who commanded the volunteer Marauders in US operations against the Japanese in Burma in 1944?

6. In which month of 1945 was the end of the war in Europe officially celebrated as V-E day?

7. What dramatic but true statement about Europe did Winston Churchill make in a speech in 1946 in Fulton, Missouri?

8. What new device did the inventor Edwin Land demonstrate to the Optical Society of America in 1947?

9. Which British composer and singer together launched in 1948 a music festival that became an annual event?

10. Who was the author of *The Second Sex*, an influential polemic published in 1949?

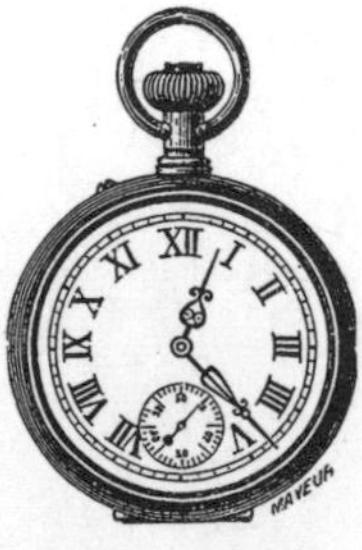

195

1. Which husband and wife were arrested in 1950 on suspicion of being Soviet spies?

2. Which artist completed in 1951 the Chapel of the Rosary at Vence, of which he had designed every detail?

3. What did x-ray crystallographer Rosalind Franklin succeed in photographing in 1952?

4. What film of 1953 was directed by Elia Kazan with Marlon Brando in the lead?

5. Whose portrait of Winston Churchill, painted for his eightieth birthday in 1954, was not well received by the sitter or his wife?

6. Which Canadian pianist won international fame in 1955 with his recording of Bach's *Goldberg Variations*?

7. Which famous marriage between an English poet and an American poet took place in 1956?

8. What name was given to the new shape of dress launched with huge success in 1957 by the designer Cristóbal Balenciaga?

9. Which Irish writer published in 1958 the autobiographical *Borstal Boy*?

10. Which prime minister of Sri Lanka was killed by a Buddhist monk in 1959, after three years in office?

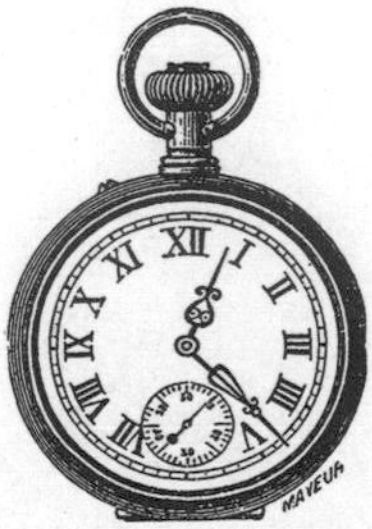

196

1. Where did South African police fire on a crowd in 1960, killing more than sixty people?

2. Whose trial began in Israel in 1961, and was broadcast live around the world from TV cameras in the court?

3. Of what did Sam Walton open the first (of very many) in Rogers, Arkansas, in 1962?

4. What began in 1963, according to Philip Larkin?

5. Which English cricketer became, in 1964, the first bowler to take 300 Test wickets?

6. What 'first' was achieved by the Soviet cosmonaut Aleksei Leonov in 1965?

7. Who moved to Bolivia in 1966 in the hope of fomenting a left-wing revolution?

8. In what film did Mike Nicholls direct Anne Bancroft and Dustin Hoffman in 1967?

9. To help which people was the movement founded, in the USA in 1968, that became known by the acronym AIM?

10. For what purpose did nearly half a million people converge on a dairy farm near Bethel, New York, in 1969?

197

1. Which film, a black comedy directed by Robert Altman in 1970, led to a very successful franchise in television and other media?

2. Of which novel by Anthony Burgess did Stanley Kubrick make a controversial film in 1971?

3. What was studied in a Tuskegee experiment that became a scandal when revealed in 1972?

4. Which prime minister, or *taoiseach*, led Ireland into the European Community in 1973?

5. Music by which US composer did choreographer Kenneth MacMillan use for his 1974 ragtime ballet *Elite Syncopations*?

6. Who developed a new element in his career in 1975, providing the sets for Stravinsky's *The Rake's Progress* at Glyndebourne?

7. Which sculptor's arrangement of bricks, *Equivalent VIII*, caused outrage in 1976 when the British public heard the price paid for it by the Tate?

8. Who was elected mayor of Paris in 1977?

9. Which English author published in 1978 his first collection of poems, *The Pleasure Steamers*?

10. What was the subject of the conference held at Lancaster House in 1979?

198

1. Which archbishop, an exponent of liberation theology, was killed in 1980 as he celebrated Mass in a chapel near his cathedral in San Salvador?

2. Which veteran Communist leader secured his position in 1981 as the real power in China's government?

3. In what context did Dustin Hoffman engage in very effective cross-dressing in 1982?

4. Which extremely successful new product was jointly launched in the USA in 1983 by Philips and Sony?

5. Of which central American country did the CIA secretly arrange for the harbours to be mined in 1984?

6. Which US television personality began in 1985 what became, and remains, the longest-running daytime television talk show?

7. Who escaped from Haiti in a US airforce jet in 1986 and went into exile in France?

8. Which eighteen-year-old deposed Martina Navratilova as world no. 1 in 1987?

9. A plane flown by which company was brought down by a terrorist bomb over Scotland in 1988?

10. What name is given to the non-violent revolution that removed the Communist Party from power in Czechoslovakia in 1989?

199

1. Who published, in 1990, the first formal proposal for the World Wide Web?

2. Whose play *The Madness of George III* was first performed at London's National Theatre in 1991?

3. Four Los Angeles policemen were acquitted in 1992 of violent assault against whom?

4. Which leader of the Medellín drugs cartel in Colombia was cornered and shot in 1993?

5. Who returned from the USA to post-Communist Russia in 1994 after living for eighteen years in Vermont?

6. Which theorem, a tantalizing puzzle for more than four centuries, was finally proved by British mathematician Andrew Wiles in 1995?

7. A fatal variant of CJD was first identified in Britain in 1996. What do the initials stand for?

8. A revised version of what song did Elton John sing in Westminster Abbey in 1997?

9. In which city was a building destroyed by US cruise missiles in 1998, because it was suspected of being a chemical factory linked to al-Qaeda?

10. What legal process came to an end in February 1999 when the Senate divided 55–45 and 50–50 on the two charges, well short of the required two-thirds majority?

200

1. Whose album *The Marshall Mathers LP* entered the US charts at no. 1 in the year of the millennium?

2. Letters carrying bacteria of what potentially lethal disease began to be posted in the USA in 2001?

3. What is the name of the 'free encyclopedia' put online by Jimmy Wales in 2001?

4. Which native of Kandahar became interim president of his country in 2002?

5. Whose presidency was brought to an end by the 2003 'Rose Revolution' in Georgia?

6. What acronym became the common name of a deadly new form of pneumonia, first reported in Hanoi in 2003?

7. Who played the eccentric aviation pioneer Howard Hughes in Martin Scorsese's 2004 film *The Aviator*?

8. In a statement that caused international outrage, who described what in 2005 as a blot that should be 'wiped off the map'?

9. Which new country declared its independence from Serbia in 2006?

10. Which long-term enemies agreed in March 2007 to share power in a reconvened assembly?

Answers

1 COUPLES

1. Dante was inspired by the sight of Beatrice (*c.* 1274).

2. Victoria and Albert (it was a mainly German custom at the time, brought into royal family life by Albert after their wedding in 1840).

3. Cleopatra, dressed as the goddess of love, arrived at Tarsus to visit Antony.

4. Richard Burton and Elizabeth Taylor (they were first married in 1964, divorced in 1970 and remarried in 1975).

5. Frankie and Johnny (the musical opened in 1904; the song was written by Hughie Cannon).

6. Robert Browning and Elizabeth Barrett (married in 1846).

7. Naples (his ship docked there in 1793; she was the wife of the British envoy, Sir William Hamilton).

8. Bonnie Parker and Clyde Barrow (in the 1967 film *Bonnie and Clyde*).

9. Hector Berlioz (fell in love with Harriet Smithson in 1827 and married her in 1833).

10. Dido and Aeneas (the first performance of Purcell's opera *Dido and Aeneas* was given in 1689 at a school for young gentlewomen in Chelsea).

2 GEORGE

1. George II (in 1727; it has been sung at the coronation of every British monarch since).

2. George Orwell (his autobiographical *Down and Out in Paris and London* was published in 1933).

3. George Grivas (from 1954).

4. George Stephenson (in 1814).

5. Georges Pompidou (in 1962).

6. George Custer (in 1876 – Custer's Last Stand, from which only a single horse, Comanche, survived).

7. George Fox (in 1655).

8. George Washington (during his expedition to the Ohio region in 1754).

9. Georges Braque (it was painted in 1908).

10. George Herbert (he died in 1633 and *The Temple* was published later in the same year).

3 TITLES IN FICTION

1. Scarlet (as punishment for her adultery she has to wear a scarlet letter; *The Scarlet Letter* was published in 1850).

2. A god (her novel *The God of Small Things* was published in 1997).

3. The lightness of being (Milan Kundera's *The Unbearable Lightness of Being* was published in 1984).

4. Paradise (*This Side of Paradise* was published in 1920).

5. Flaubert (*Flaubert's Parrot* was published in 1984).

6. A rainbow (his novel *Gravity's Rainbow* was published in 1973).

7. *Tristesse*, or sadness (*Bonjour Tristesse*, her first novel, was published in 1954, when she was nineteen).

8. Cement (*The Cement Garden* was published in 1978).

9. A rain king (his novel *Henderson the Rain King* was published in 1959).

10. Love (*The Pursuit of Love* was published in 1945).

4 LONDON

1. Sarah Siddons (in 1782).

2. Boxing, or prizefighting (kicking, gouging, scratching and head-butting were also banned in the London Prize Ring Rules of 1838).

3. Catholic emancipation (six days of riots were prompted by the Protestant extremist Lord George Gordon in 1780).

4. Marie Stopes (with her husband, in 1921).

5. The V-2 rocket (the V-1 flying bombs, or doodlebugs, had begun landing in London four months earlier).

6. Claude Monet (in 1870).

7. Pocahontas (the wife of John Rolfe, in 1616).

8. The Great Stink.

9. Sylvie Guillem.

10. John Constable (in 1820).

5 BLUE AND GREEN

1. Celadons (from about 1100).

2. The Blue Mosque (commissioned by the sultan Ahmed I and begun in 1609).

3. *Sir Gawain and the Green Knight* (written in about 1375).

4. Rose (his Blue period evolved into his Rose period in 1905).

5. As the location of the prime meridian, or zero° longitude (in 1884).

6. The Bluebell Girls (from 1932; Margaret Kelly was herself known as 'Miss Bluebell').

7. Graham Greene (in *Brighton Rock*, published in 1938).

8. *The Blue Angel* (shot in both German and English in 1930).

9. In Libya (it contains the thoughts of Muammar al-Gaddafi, first published in 1975).

10. Gerrit Rietveld (in 1918).

6 INVENTIONS

1. The pendulum (in 1656, in The Hague).

2. The telephone (Meucci's patent was filed in 1871; the first coherent spoken message was conveyed by Bell's machine in 1876).

3. The sternpost rudder (a rudder which is an integral part of the ship, introduced in about 1200).

4. They were the first made by exposing a negative, from which a positive print could be made (in 1835).

5. Parchment ('*pergamena*' in Latin, first used in about 170 BC).

6. The first PC, or personal computer (launched in 1981 as the IBM PC 5150, with a chip by Intel and software by Microsoft).

7. Bifocals (in 1784, when Franklin was irritated by needing two pairs of glasses).

8. The stethoscope (in 1816).

9. The cotton gin (invented in the USA in 1793).

10. The pressure cooker (developed in 1685 by Papin, a French scientist working in England, as part of his experiments with steam).

7 SIX

1. The six *Brandenburg Concertos* (in 1721).

2. *The Full Monty* (in which they became male strippers, in 1997).

3. Calais (in 1347).

4. The European Coal and Steel Community (formed in 1951, followed by the European Economic Community in 1957).

5. The Old Testament (*c.* AD 245).

6. An author (Pirandello wrote *Six Characters in Search of an Author* in 1921).

7. Continental drift (beginning about 200 million years ago).

8. Ulster, or Northern Ireland (created by the Government of Ireland Act in 1920).

9. C. B. Fry (in 1901).

10. Joseph Haydn (Op. 1 was published in 1764).

8 BRIDGE

1. San Francisco (by the Golden Gate Bridge, completed in 1937).

2. Robert Stephenson (in 1850).

3. The Tay (the Tay Bridge disaster occurred in 1879).

4. The Ponte Vecchio ('Old Bridge').

5. Brooklands.

6. Ely Culbertson (from 1926 – auction bridge dates from earlier than that).

7. *The Bridge of San Luis Rey* (1927).

8. Longbridge (in 1905).

9. Marco Polo (the Marco Polo Bridge Incident, in 1937, was a clash between Japanese and Chinese troops that was used by Japan as a pretext to attack China).

10. Britain's largest ever theft took place in Tonbridge in 2006, when £53 million was stolen from a Securitas depot.

9 VIRGIN

1. Michelangelo (in 1499).

2. The Virgin Mary (who was thus born without original sin, a doctrine of faith for Roman Catholics since 1854; the doctrine applying to the birth of Jesus is the Virgin Birth).

3. The Aztec Virgin (she appeared to an Indian in 1531 and told him she was 'one of his kind').

4. *Like a Virgin* (1984).

5. The *Wilton Diptych* (in London's National Gallery, commissioned in about 1387).

6. The Eiffel Tower in Paris (in 1915, transmitted from the US Navy's radio tower in Arlington).

7. Bloomsbury (the Stephen sisters became Virginia Woolf and Vanessa Bell; the Bloomsbury Group gathered at their home from about 1905).

8. Elephant dung (used as part of the decorative element of the picture, in 1996).

9. *Who's Afraid of Virginia Woolf?* (play, 1962; film, 1966).

10. She was the first English child to be born in America, on Roanoke Island (in 1587 – but she and her entire settler community had perished within three years).

10 LITERATURE

1. Samuel Pepys (as described in the very first entry in his diary).

2. His patron, Maecenas (*c.* 34 BC).

3. Constantine Cavafy (from 1892).

4. Sa'di (the poem was published in 1257).

5. Christopher Marlowe and William Shakespeare (in 1564; Marlowe was the older by two months).

6. Fleur Adcock (in 1964).

7. Percy Bysshe Shelley (in 1811).

8. Marco Polo (presented to Kublai Khan in 1275).

9. His own suicide (the Samurai ritual of *seppuku* involves slashing open one's own stomach).

10. *The Satanic Verses* (published in 1988; the fatwa was issued in 1989).

11 FLORA

1. Henry James (his novel *Daisy Miller* was published in 1879).

2. The 1630s (the tulip craze lasted approximately from 1633 to 1637).

3. Mark Morris (this dance company was set up in 1990 to tour ballet nationally and internationally).

4. Mao Zedong, who in his Hundred Flowers Campaign invited criticism and then locked up the critics (in 1957).

5. Teddy's Bear (in 1902; it was the ancestor of the infinite number of dolls subsequently known as teddy bears).

6. e. e. cummings (the collection was published in 1923).

7. Daisy Ashford (she wrote the book in 1890; it was published in 1919).

8. Hemlock, or *Conium maculatum* (used in ancient Athens to induce a slow death).

9. Charles Baudelaire (the collection was published in 1857).

10. The Battle of Worcester (after this defeat in 1651, he is said to have hidden from the parliamentary forces in an oak tree at Boscobel, Shropshire).

12 FAUNA

1. Napoleon (in George Orwell's *Animal Farm*, published in 1945).

2. The opening of the Colosseum in Rome, presided over by the emperor Titus.

3. In the air, in a Montgolfier balloon (they were the first living passengers in any form of aircraft, at Versailles in 1783).

4. The hippopotamus (*c*. 5000 BC).

5. Llamas (*c*. 1500).

6. The Barnum and Bailey Circus (Jumbo was billed as 'the world's largest elephant', from about 1882).

7. The Roslin Institute, in Edinburgh (in 1996).

8. La Brea tar pit (the fossils date from over 15,000 years ago, and there are some traces of human activity).

9. The hamster (the original was captured and bred from in about 1930).

10. Przewalski's horse (a very rare example of the wild breed from which the horse was domesticated, discovered in 1875).

13 ARCHAEOLOGY

1. *Homo erectus* (about 1.6 million years ago).

2. Jericho (which dates from about 8000 BC).

3. The eighteenth century (digging began in 1748).

4. *The Epic of Gilgamesh* (the clay tablets date from about 650 BC, though the epic itself is much earlier).

5. Ur (in modern Iraq, dating from about 2500 BC and discovered in the 1920s).

6. Wheat (in the Middle East, from about 8000 BC).

7. Sheep (in northern Iraq, from about 8000 BC).

8. Japan (from about 5000 BC).

9. Seahenge (dating from about 2000 BC, and revealed by gradual erosion of the coast).

10. Çatal Höyük (dating from about 6500 BC).

14 ARCHITECTS

1. Buckminster Fuller (for the World's Fair in Montreal in 1967).

2. Albert Speer (designed the Zeppelintribüne, the Nuremberg parade ground, in 1934).

3. Daniel Libeskind (the project was completed in 1987).

4. The competition to design the Sydney Opera House.

5. Filippo Brunelleschi (in 1418).

6. The Festival of Britain in 1951 (the Skylon was designed by Arnold Powell and John Moya).

7. Basil Spence (in 1951).

8. Brasilia (in 1957).

9. Antoni Gaudí (died in 1926).

10. Eliel Saarinen (father of Eero Saarinen, in 1904).

15 ARMIES

1. At Xi'an, China (he was a Qin emperor, buried in 206 BC, accompanied by an army of life-size terracotta soldiers).

2. Alexander Nevsky (after winning a battle on the River Neva in 1240).

3. The Rubicon (his crossing of the Rubicon launched a civil war in 49 BC).

4. The Burma National Army, commanded by Aung San (in 1945).

5. The New Model Army (formed in 1645).

6. Stendhal (whose real name was Marie Henri Beyle; in 1812).

7. Australian and New Zealand Army Corps (for ever associated with the Gallipoli campaign of 1915).

8. The Prussian Army (in 1848).

9. Stanley Spencer (from 1914).

10. Australia's Salvation Army (in 1900).

16 ASTRONOMY AND SPACE

1. Men and animals on the moon (in 1835).

2. Percival Lowell (built the Lowell Observatory in 1894).

3. The proposal that our galaxy rotates (in 1926).

4. Nicolaus Copernicus, whose *De Revolutionibus Orbium Coelestium* (*On the Revolution of the Celestial Spheres*) was published in 1543.

5. Tahiti (in 1769; this was the main purpose of his voyage to the Pacific).

6. The Crab Nebula (observed in China and Japan in 1054).

7. 1970 (a commitment made in 1961 and achieved ahead of target by *Apollo 11* in 1969).

8. Halley's Comet (which appeared in 1066).

9. Luna (*Luna 1* was the first in the series).

10. Andromeda (proved in 1924 to be a galaxy, the nearest spiral galaxy to our own).

17 BIRDS

1. Hampstead, in his own garden ('Ode to a Nightingale' was published in 1820).

2. Russell Crowe (in 2000).

3. *Early Bird* (Intelsat I).

4. Edgar Allan Poe (the collection was published in 1845).

5. A peacock (*The White Peacock* was published in 1911).

6. Clarence Birdseye (who introduced frozen food, launching Birdseye Seafoods in New York in 1924).

7. Baghdad (*c.* 1050).

8. *The Blue Bird* (premiered at the Moscow Art Theatre).

9. Flann O'Brien (the book was published in 1939).

10. Konrad Lorenz (*c.* 1935).

18 BISHOPS

1. The Bishops' Wars (of 1639 and 1640, in protest against the attempt by Charles I and Archbishop Laud to impose an Anglican hierarchy).

2. James Ussher, Archbishop of Armagh (he published his chronology in two parts in 1650 and 1654).

3. Liberation theology (from 1968).

4. Elizabeth Bishop.

5. St Andrews (in 1546).

6. Giovanni Battista Tiepolo (from 1751).

7. Rhodesia (subsequently Zimbabwe).

8. Archbishop Makarios III (elected president in 1960).

9. St Augustine (St Augustine of Canterbury, as opposed to the earlier St Augustine of Hippo).

10. Maurice Bishop (executed after a coup).

19 DISASTERS AND ATROCITIES

1. Thera, or Santorini (*c.* 1525 BC).

2. Chechen terrorists (in Moscow in 2002).

3. A pandemic of influenza (which caused about 30 million deaths in 1918–19).

4. Rome, after the tribes had pushed south through the Alps.

5. Union Carbide (more than 2000 deaths resulted from the 1984 accident).

6. *Candide* (his satire on optimism, prompted by the earthquake of 1755 and published in 1759).

7. Virginia Tech (in 2007).

8. Darwin (in 1974).

9. The Black Death.

10. Krakatoa.

20 COURTS

1. The Royal Court Theatre, London (in 1956).

2. Margaret Court (in 1963).

3. She was the first female member of the US Supreme Court (appointed by Ronald Reagan in 1981).

4. Miles Standish (*The Courtship of Miles Standish* was published in 1858).

5. A real-tennis court (at Versailles, in 1789).

6. Diego Velázquez (court painter to Philip IV from 1623).

7. The Appomattox Court House (Lee's surrender ending the American Civil War, in 1865).

8. The Battle of Agincourt (in 1415).

9. The Prix Goncourt (first awarded in 1903, according to the will of Edmond de Goncourt, brother of Jules).

10. Courtly love (from about 1120).

21 BLACK AND RED

1. Stendhal (*Le Rouge et le Noir*, or *The Red and the Black*, was published in 1830).

2. Britain (during the Boer War, at Stromberg, Magersfontein and Colenso, in 1899).

3. Jelly Roll Morton (and the Red Hot Peppers, in 1926).

4. The red corpuscles (through a microscope that he had built himself, in 1674).

5. Dante (as a member of the White faction, in 1402).

6. The Red Cross (established in 1863 by Henri Dunant, who had been present at Solferino in 1859).

7. Kasimir Malevich (in 1915).

8. The Red River Rebellion (in 1869; Manitoba became a province in 1870).

9. Merce Cunningham (in 1953).

10. Aldo Moro (in 1978).

22 STONE

1. The Stone of Scone (removed from Scotland in 1296 and returned to Scone in 1996).

2. Mary Wollstonecraft (the book was published in 1792).

3. The Neolithic (meaning 'new stone') Revolution, sometimes also called the Agricultural Revolution (beginning in about 8000 BC in the Middle East).

4. William Gladstone (prime minister 1868–74, 1880–85, 1886 and 1892–4).

5. Lithography (in 1798, while he was experimenting with the incompatibility of grease and water on stone).

6. The Stonewall Riots.

7. St Stephen was stoned, outside the city wall of Jerusalem (in about 35 BC).

8. David Livingstone (in 1855).

9. Stonehenge (the novel was published in 1891).

10. Keystone Studio (which was set up in 1912 and produced the Keystone Kops).

23 CASTLES

1. *The Castle of Otranto* (1764).

2. Franz Kafka (he died in 1924, the book was published in 1926).

3. An eisteddfod (in 1176).

4. Edward I (from 1283).

5. Fotheringay Castle (in 1587).

6. *Duke Bluebeard's Castle* (in 1918).

7. Krak des Chevaliers (in Syria; building began in 1142).

8. Martello towers (built in 1803; their name derives from a similar tower at Mortella in Corsica).

9. The castle at Colditz (in 1940).

10. Defenestration (two Habsburg regents were thrown out of a window by discontented Bohemians in 1618).

24 SPORT BEFORE 1900

1. Croquet (the championship was organized in 1877 by the All-England Croquet Club at Wimbledon).

2. US football (the payment was made in 1892).

3. Boxing (the academy opened in 1740).

4. Veterans of the American Civil War (the Association was founded in 1871; the Civil War lasted from 1861 to 1865).

5. Polo (*c.* 550 BC).

6. Baseball (in 1845).

7. The Ashes (because the *Sporting Times* said the Australians would take home with them 'the ashes of English cricket').

8. Sumo wrestling (the first competition was supposedly held in 23 BC).

9. Cincinnati (in 1869).

10. Motor racing (in 1894).

25 FLIGHT

1. Over the South Pole (in a Ford Tri-Motor in 1929).

2. Ferdinand Zeppelin (his first dirigible, or airship, first flew in 1900).

3. A jet aircraft (tested in Germany in 1939).

4. William Boeing (in 1916).

5. Ghana (in 1979).

6. Benjamin Franklin (in 1732; he survived the experiment).

7. Toulouse (in 2005).

8. Rudolf Hess (parachuting from his Messerschmitt, in 1941).

9. Hermann Goering (he became commander of the elite Richthofen Squadron in 1918).

10. Amy Johnson (in 1930).

26 BOOK

1. *Baby and Child Care* (1946).

2. Andrea Palladio (*c.* 1570).

3. Judaism (the book was written in about AD 930).

4. Noah Webster (in 1783).

5. Italy (*c.* 1300).

6. *The Golden Notebook.*

7. All Confucian books (unless of practical use, in 213 BC).

8. The Book of Mormon (in 1830).

9. *A Book of Nonsense* (1846).

10. *The Pillow Book* of Sei Shōnagon (written in about AD 995).

27 WINTER AND ICE

1. Frost fairs on the Thames (the narrow arches of the bridge had held back the tide enabling thick ice to form, impossible after its demolition in 1831).

2. Basketball (in 1891).

3. Louis Agassiz.

4. 'The Winter King' (he reigned only from 1619 to 1620 before being forced to flee).

5. *Bolero* (used by Jayne Torvill and Christopher Dean in 1984).

6. The 'winter of discontent' (1978–9).

7. Maxim de Winter (in Daphne du Maurier's novel, published in 1938).

8. René Descartes (in 1650).

9. Leon Trotsky (killed in 1940 by a Soviet agent).

10. The Winter Palace in Petrograd (now St Petersburg again) in 1917.

28 CITY AND TOWN

1. The massive aqueduct known as the Pont du Gard (*c.* AD 20).

2. The Toltecs (from about AD 950).

3. Granada (in 1492).

4. Babylon (in 689 BC).

5. *On the Town* (1949).

6. Machu Picchu (rediscovered in about 1911).

7. Indus civilization (*c.* 2500 BC).

8. Salt Lake City (selected by the Mormon leader in 1847).

9. The first garden city (Letchworth was begun in 1903).

10. George Balanchine (in 1948).

29 NOVELTIES

1. The great tenor Enrico Caruso (but it was not a success because of the poor quality of the broadcast).

2. Semaphore or telegraph (he invented both words, in 1791).

3. Spam (the first cans went on sale in 1937).

4. Czechoslovakia (Czechs and Slovaks united under this name in 1918 and separated peacefully into the Czech Republic and Slovakia in 1993).

5. Chess (first played in India in about AD 550).

6. The Gregorian calendar (the Julian calendar was by then eleven days out, so 3 September had to be renamed 14 September).

7. He was a freed slave, who had been captured as a child in Africa and later settled in England (his book was published in 1789).

8. The multi-talented Benjamin Franklin.

9. Instant coffee (in 1901).

10. Claude Monet (together they developed '*plein-air*' painting and Impressionism, in 1869).

30 CANINES

1. *Reservoir Dogs* (1992).

2. Jack London (the novel was published in 1903).

3. Rabies (the child had been bitten by a rabid dog, in 1885).

4. James Wolfe (he lost his life there in the battle which won Quebec for the British, in 1759).

5. The first of the Lascaux caves and their famous prehistoric paintings (discovered in about 1940).

6. Bulldog Drummond (who made his first appearance in Sapper's 1920 novel of that name).

7. Germany (in 1916, to guide soldiers blinded in the First World War).

8. Giacomo Balla (in 1912).

9. Wolfe Tone.

10. Anton van Leeuwenhoek (in 1677).

31 BRITAIN

1. Manchester (magistrates ordered troops to fire on a crowd of demonstrators, in 1819, killing eleven and wounding 500).

2. The Liberals and the Social Democratic Party (SDP), in 1988.

3. Henry Moore (in 1940, when he was working as an official war artist, in his series of drawings in the Underground).

4. The discovery in peat of the well-preserved body now known as Lindow Man (he died in about 50 BC, possibly a sacrificial victim of the Druids, and is now in the British Museum).

5. Arnold Wesker (*Chicken Soup with Barley* was first performed in 1958, followed by *Roots* in 1959 and *I'm Talking about Jerusalem* in 1960).

6. Pulsar (identified in 1967 by Jocelyn Bell and Anthony Hewish).

7. *Life on Earth* (first broadcast in 1978).

8. Oliver Cromwell (even though he had died in 1658; his body was exhumed for the occasion in 1661, after the Restoration of the monarchy in 1660).

9. London Bridge (construction began in 1176).

10. 'Colonel Bogey' (written by Kenneth Alford in 1913; it was used as a musical theme in *The Bridge on the River Kwai* in 1957).

32 DECEIT

1. The extent of US involvement in Vietnam (the Pentagon Papers were published in 1971).

2. Lambert Simnel (he was captured in 1487 and lived until 1535).

3. Ernest (which turns out also to be his real name in Oscar Wilde's *The Importance of Being Earnest*, first performed in 1895).

4. Ossian (the forgery by James MacPherson enjoyed great though brief success).

5. Their real names were Charlotte and Emily Brontë (*Jane Eyre* and *Wuthering Heights* were published in 1847 under the respective pseudonyms Currer and Ellis Bell).

6. Ivan the Terrible (False Dmitry I raised an army to claim the throne in 1604, False Dmitry II in 1608 and False Dmitry III in 1612).

7. Piltdown Man (his forgery of a fossilized human skull, supposedly found in 1912 in a gravel pit at Piltdown, East Sussex).

8. Seventeen-year-old Thomas Chatterton (he died in 1770, after acquiring fame as the discoverer of supposedly medieval documents and poems that he had written himself; the painting dates from 1856).

9. The Zinoviev Letter (a forgery instructing British Communists to prepare for revolution, widely believed in 1924).

10. Felix Krull (in *Confessions of Felix Krull, Confidence Man*, an incomplete novel published in 1955).

33 MOON

1. 'Shine On, Harvest Moon'.

2. Ban Ki-moon (a South Korean, in 2007).

3. *Apollo 8* (the first spacecraft to go into orbit round the moon, in 1968).

4. Sun Myung Moon (in 1954; his followers soon became known as the Moonies).

5. Drive a vehicle (the Lunar Rover, in 1971).

6. Saturn (in 1655).

7. *Dangerous Moonlight* (in 1940).

8. The moons of Jupiter (in 1610).

9. Octavio Paz (the collection was published in 1933, when he was nineteen).

10. Georges Méliès (in 1902).

34 HERO

1. Tristram Shandy (in the first of Laurence Sterne's two volumes, published in 1759).

2. Charles Pooter (in his fictional diary by George and Weedon Grossmith, published in 1892).

3. John Paul Jones (in 1779).

4. Thomas Cole (in 1827).

5. Albania (Skanderbeg won several victories against the Turks, beginning in 1443).

6. Herodotus (writing in about 460 BC).

7. Giuseppe Verdi (in 1901).

8. *The Rape of the Lock* (1712).

9. Hero of Alexandria (a Greek scientist working in the city in about AD 75).

10. Dorian Gray (in Oscar Wilde's novel *The Picture of Dorian Gray*, published in 1891).

35 CAPITALS

1. Vienna.

2. The Potomac (selected in 1790 as the site for Washington, DC).

3. Samarkand (in 1398).

4. The Olmecs (La Venta became the capital in about 900 BC).

5. On the Tigris (in 312 BC).

6. Kyoto (in AD 794).

7. St Petersburg (by Peter the Great, in 1703).

8. Rome (capital of the newly unified kingdom of Italy).

9. The Aztecs (*c.* 1345).

10. On the Nile, in AD 969 (the name Al Kahira has now been shortened in English to Cairo).

36 FORD

1. The Ford Model T.

2. Richard Nixon, Ford's predecessor as US president, was pardoned for any part he may have played in the Watergate affair (in 1974).

3. Wexford (captured in 1169) and Waterford (captured in 1170).

4. Sir Walter Scott (from 1822).

5. Bedford (from 1661).

6. Marconi (from 1922).

7. Mary Pickford (in 1919).

8. Richard Arkwright (in 1771).

9. The Morris Oxford (produced from 1913 at William Morris's factory at Cowley, near Oxford).

10. *Alice's Adventures in Wonderland* (told in improvised form by Charles Dodgson, better known as Lewis Carroll, to Alice Liddell in 1862, and published in 1865).

37 NEW

1. New Amsterdam (it was renamed in 1666, after the British acquired it from the Dutch).

2. St Paul (they are his epistles, of which the Epistle to the Thessalonians is the earliest, written in about AD 50).

3. HIV (discovered in 1983).

4. George IV (in 1822).

5. *Turbinia* (broke the water speed record in 1897, while Queen Victoria was reviewing her fleet).

6. Robert Owen (in 1812).

7. Spain (at Córdoba, in AD 756).

8. John Reith (in 1922).

9. Jesse James (he had allowed the man into his home).

10. The Pharisees (*c.* 140 BC).

38 JOHN

1. John Buchan (the book was published in 1910).

2. John Logie Baird (in 1926).

3. John Betjeman (the poem was published in 1960).

4. Samuel Johnson and James Boswell (in 1763).

5. John Adams (*Nixon in China* premiered in 1987).

6. Sir John Moore (in 1809, as described in the poem 'The Burial of Sir John Moore at Corunna', 1816, by Charles Wolfe).

7. John Huss, or Jan Hus (in 1402).

8. Admiral John Byng (in 1757, for 'neglect of duty' in failing to relieve Minorca in 1756).

9. John André (in 1780).

10. Magic Johnson (he joined the Lakers in 1980).

39 NORTH AMERICA

1. Nova Scotia (around 1783, when the independence of the British colonies was fully established).

2. Nat Turner (fifty-nine white people were killed during the revolt, in 1831, provoking new repressive legislation).

3. Leif Ericsson (*c.* AD 1000).

4. The Huron (in 1648).

5. Elijah Muhammad.

6. Hawaii, in the North Pacific (which joined the Union as the fiftieth state in 1959).

7. 'Let us now praise famous men' (the book was published in 1941, with text by Agee and photographs by Evans).

8. Alex Haley (in 1976).

9. Ohio (the mounds date from around AD 1000).

10. Aboriginal title to land (in 1973).

40 HORROR

1. The Dust Bowl (in *The Grapes of Wrath*, published in 1939).

2. Cambodia.

3. *Slaughterhouse-Five* (1969), by Kurt Vonnegut.

4. William Gladstone (the pamphlet was published in 1876).

5. Edgar Wallace (who was closely involved with the 1933 film).

6. *Little Shop of Horrors*.

7. *Dr Jekyll and Mr Hyde*, by Robert Louis Stevenson (the film was made from a popular stage production of the book).

8. *The Exorcist* (1973).

9. John Singer Sargent (in 1919).

10. *Carrie* (1973).

41 PRISON

1. At the Bay of Pigs (the prisoners were Cuban exiles, captured in 1961 and released in 1962).

2. Ezra Pound (the book-length poem was published in 1948).

3. *Le Morte d'Arthur* (an English account of the French tales of King Arthur, written in 1469).

4. Margaret Sanger (in 1916).

5. Konrad Adenauer (in 1955).

6. Maya Angelou (*I Know Why the Caged Bird Sings* was published in 1970).

7. The *Altmark* (in a Norwegian fjord in 1940).

8. John Howard (in 1773).

9. Francis I (in 1525).

10. Shah Jahan (by Aurangzeb, from 1658).

42 AFRICA

1. Morocco (by taking Marrakech in 1269).

2. Winston Churchill (at the Battle of Omdurman in the Sudan in 1898; he described his experiences in *The River War*, published in 1899).

3. The Dance Theatre of Harlem (in 1992).

4. Leander Jameson (led the Jameson Raid in 1895).

5. Frelimo (from 1962 until independence was won in 1975).

6. The Mamelukes (who had served the Turks as slaves, from 1250).

7. The Boers (in the Transvaal).

8. On the Rosetta Stone, in the British Museum (carved in 196 BC, with an inscription from the reign of Ptolemy V).

9. She was a female pharaoh (she came to the Egyptian throne in about 1490 BC).

10. Bantu (from about 1480).

43 ANIMALS

1. The suffragettes (they were released and later rearrested, in response to their hunger strikes while in prison).

2. *The Scapegoat* (1855).

3. To provide pasture for sheep (from 1846).

4. William Cody (who from 1867 slaughtered thousands of buffalo to feed construction workers on the Union Pacific Railroad).

5. The zodiac (known by the Greeks from about 550 BC as '*zodiakos kyklos*').

6. The Battle of the Camel (in AD 656).

7. The Indian Mutiny (Muslim and Hindu sepoys objected in 1857 to the animal fat, potentially pig or cow, that was used to grease new cartridges).

8. The first of the Dead Sea Scrolls (in 1947).

9. T'ang dynasty (AD 618–907).

10. Edward Muybridge (in 1887).

1. The Exchequer (from the checkered table used to make calculations, from about 1170).

2. From the tradition that it was translated by seventy scholars (in Alexandria in about 280 BC; the Latin for 'seventy' is '*septuaginta*').

3. Ivan the Terrible (he was crowned in 1547).

4. Jan Zizka (*c.* 1422, during the Hussite rebellion against the emperor Sigismund and Pope Martin V).

5. *The Little Red Book* (first published in 1964).

6. The Grito de Dolores, or Cry of Dolores (in 1810).

7. The Bill of Rights (ratified in 1791).

8. Monster meetings (in 1842).

9. The Pleiades, or La Pléiade (their manifesto was written by Joachim du Bellay in 1549).

10. Spain (in 1810).

45 CHINA

1. Chinese emperor (placed on the throne in 1908 – he was also the last of the Qing dynasty).

2. 'Capitalist roaders' (in 1966).

3. Bronze (chopsticks have been found in Shang dynasty tombs, dating from about 1400 BC).

4. Tiananmen Square (it is one of the entrances to the Forbidden City; Mao Zedong stood here in 1949 to proclaim the new People's Republic of China).

5. The first Mongol emperor, Kublai Khan (in 1271).

6. Chiang Kai-shek (who set up the National Government in Nanjing in 1928; the new spelling follows the *pinyin* system, adopted in China in 1979).

7. The Long March (the Chinese Communist Army moved from Jiangxi to Shaanxi to escape from Kuomintang forces).

8. The Boxer Rising, or Rebellion (in 1900).

9. Lord Macartney (to the emperor Qianlong in 1792).

10. The Shang dynasty.

46 STUDENTS

1. The Pre-Raphaelite Brotherhood (formed by Dante Gabriel Rossetti, Holman Hunt and John Everett Millais in 1848).

2. Olivier Messiaen (in 1942).

3. The enrolment of women as degree students (in 1837).

4. Lenin's elder brother (Alexander was executed in 1887).

5. The Taliban (meaning 'students', in this case of the Koran; in 1994).

6. Zuleika Dobson (in Max Beerbohm's *Zuleika Dobson*, published in 1911).

7. Kent State University (in 1970).

8. Richard Rodgers and Lorenz Hart (in 1920).

9. Matteo Ricci (he arrived in China in 1583).

10. Octavian (in 44 BC; he was known as Augustus Caesar after 27 BC).

47 SUN

1. Bees (as demonstrated by Frisch in 1949).

2. *The Sun Also Rises* (1926).

3. *Saturday Night and Sunday Morning* (1968).

4. *Never on Sunday* (1960).

5. Sun Records (in 1964; Elvis Presley was the truck driver).

6. Louis XIV, later known as the Sun King (in a ballet of 1653).

7. The Colossus of Rhodes (one of the seven wonders of the world, erected in 292 BC).

8. The Milky Way (formed about 4.6 billion years ago).

9. Impressionism (coined in 1874 by the critic Louis Leroy to ridicule Monet's painting *Impression, Sunrise*).

10. Port Sunlight (built in Merseyside in 1888 beside his Sunlight Soap factory).

48 THEATRE

1. The Theatre (built in 1576).

2. The Theatre of the Absurd (in 1950).

3. The operating theatre (he introduced carbolic acid and antiseptic surgery in 1865).

4. Pyotr Stolypin (in 1911).

5. Japanese No theatre (in 1374; the shogun was Yoshimitsu).

6. Epidaurus (built around 340 BC).

7. Edward Gordon Craig (the manifesto was published in 1905).

8. The Wurlitzer (produced by Rudolph Wurlitzer's company).

9. John Wilkes Booth (in 1865).

10. Fred Astaire (in 1906).

49 TOMBS

1. Jacob Epstein (in 1912).

2. The Persian emperor Cyrus the Great, or Cyrus II (buried in about 530 BC).

3. San Sepolcro (he worked there around 1450).

4. Delhi (the tomb was completed in 1573).

5. Mali (the graves date from about 1200).

6. Julius II (the tomb was commissioned in 1505, but it was so elaborate that it was never completed).

7. In Westminster Abbey (the body, from one of the unmarked graves in a British war cemetery, was placed there in 1919).

8. Philip of Macedon, the father of Alexander the Great (the tombs were excavated in about 1977).

9. At Saqqara (the tomb was built in about 2620 BC).

10. A beehive tomb (dating from about 1400 BC).

50 NEWS

1. Prester John (a figure of fantasy, rumours of whose existence were first spread in 1145 by a bishop in the Latin Kingdom of Jerusalem).

2. Benito Mussolini (in 1914 – Italy joined the War on the Allied side in 1915).

3. The publication of cartoons of Muhammad (in 2005).

4. The *Illustrated London News* (it first included chromolithographs in its Christmas issue of 1855).

5. Nathan Mayer Rothschild (the great banker, whose communication system was more efficient than the government's).

6. William Cobbett (in 1802).

7. Germany (news sheets appeared in Augsburg and Strasbourg in 1609).

8. Roger Casement (in 1903 – he was executed in 1916 for treason, as an Irish rebel).

9. The Stamp Act (1765).

10. Printing on a steam press (in 1814).

51 UNKNOWN

1. The Indus civilization (*c.* 2500 BC).

2. Wilhelm Roentgen (in 1895).

3. Michael Ventris (he deciphered it in 1952).

4. Percival Lowell (predicted the planet in 1905; Pluto was discovered in 1930).

5. In Arlington National Cemetery (the first of America's 'unknown soldiers' was placed there in 1921).

6. Arthur Zimmermann (sent the Zimmermann telegram in 1917).

7. Australia (from Terra Australis Incognita, used after the discovery of the Solomon Islands in 1568).

8. Vincent van Gogh (in the asylum 1889–90, died later in 1890).

9. Mozart's *Requiem Mass* (the commission was given and accepted in the year of Mozart's own death, 1791).

10. Huddie Ledbetter, now better known as Leadbelly (in 1933).

52 WINNERS AND LOSERS

1. Aeschylus (who had won for the first time in 484 BC).

2. Aung San (leader of the Anti-Fascist People's Freedom League).

3. Antony and Cleopatra (at the battle of Actium).

4. David Garrick (after the battle of Quiberon Bay).

5. Eddie Merckx (in 1978).

6. The Afghan mujaheddin (in 1988).

7. As a racing schooner, in sailing contests (from 1921).

8. Kenneth Kaunda (he had been president since 1964).

9. Benjamin Netanyahu (in Israel).

10. Napoleon (defeating an Egyptian army in 1798).

53 WHITE

1. Jainism (*c.* 50 BC).

2. The *Titanic.*

3. Whitehall (outside the Banqueting House, in 1649).

4. John Adams (in 1810).

5. Heavyweight boxing (in the so-called White Hope era, boxing promoters were looking for a white man to defeat Jack Johnson, the first black heavyweight champion; Willard did so in 1915).

6. White Russians, led by Lavr Kornilov.

7. He drowned when the *White Ship* struck a rock off Cherbourg (in 1120).

8. The Battle of the White Mountain (in 1620).

9. The White Company (Hawkwood was appointed Captain General of Florence in 1378).

10. American Indians (he sketched the Secotan during the 1585 expedition to Roanoke Island led by Richard Grenville).

54 HORSES

1. *National Velvet* (1944).

2. A vacuum (sixteen horses couldn't separate two iron hemispheres held together by an internal vacuum, in Regensburg in 1654).

3. Hernando Cortés (landed in Mexico in 1519 with 600 men, 16 horses and about 20 guns).

4. *The Four Horsemen of the Apocalypse* (1921).

5. The Palio (a regular annual event since about 1250).

6. At the Derby (she was the suffragette who was killed when she threw herself in front of the king's horse in 1913).

7. George Stubbs (who set up a studio in London in 1758).

8. *'Dada'* (selected from a dictionary by Tristan Tzara and friends in Zurich).

9. Olympia (in 1907).

10. The Byerley Turk (three sires brought to England in about 1710, the ancestors of all thoroughbred racehorses).

55 SCOTLAND

1. Macbeth (killed Duncan in 1040).

2. Peter Maxwell Davies (in 1977).

3. The French wrote Stuart rather than Stewart (when Mary Queen of Scots married the heir to the French throne in 1558) and the new spelling survived.

4. John Duns, known as Duns Scotus (though he was admired as the 'subtle doctor' in his own time, about 1300, the name 'duns' was later applied to foolish pedants, by humanist philosophers opposed to his methods).

5. Glencoe (in 1692).

6. James Hepburn, the Earl of Bothwell (her husband, Darnley, was murdered in 1567; she married Bothwell three months later).

7. The Battle of Culloden (in which he and his 5000 Scots were convincingly defeated by the king's forces in 1746, thwarting all hopes of his dynasty recovering the British throne).

8. It was a tug powered by steam (designed by William Symington and put to work on the Forth and Clyde Canal).

9. The Covenanters (from the National Covenant, by which they agreed in 1638 to oppose Charles I's reforms of the Church of Scotland).

10. Tartan or Highland dress (banned immediately after the Forty-Five Rebellion had been brought to an end).

56 WILD

1. Henry Fielding (*The Life of Jonathan Wild the Great* was published in 1743).

2. William Gladstone (in 1892, during his fourth and final spell as Britain's prime minister).

3. The Indus civilization (*c.* 2000 BC).

4. Billy Wilder (in 1959).

5. The steppes of central Asia (from about 3000 BC).

6. Thornton Wilder (the play opened on Broadway in 1938).

7. James Abbot McNeill Whistler (from about 1881).

8. Maurice Sendak (the book was published in 1963).

9. '*Fauves*' (the critic was reviewing a 1905 exhibition in Paris).

10. The Wild West Show (launched by Cody, better known as Buffalo Bill, in 1883).

57 THE UNITED STATES

1. Oklahoma City (in 1995).

2. The Shakers (known as the 'Shaking Quakers').

3. To limit the freedom granted to the Negroes by the victorious North (in 1865).

4. Brook Farm (established in 1841).

5. Tea (in 1770 – prompting the Boston Tea Party in 1773).

6. Louisiana (he called it this in honour of Louis XIV after travelling the river's length and claiming the entire region for France, in 1682).

7. The XYZ Affair (so called because the agents who had asked for bribes in negotiations with America were concealed behind these letters in the report that revealed the scandal).

8. Fire (in 1911 nearly 150 garment-workers died in a fire at the company's factory).

9. Lewis Mumford (the book was published in 1938).

10. Abraham Lincoln (the poem was published in *Sequel to Drum-Taps* in 1866).

58 WIVES

1. Franz Schubert (*Die Schöne Müllerin*, or *The Beautiful Miller's Wife*, 1823).

2. Arthur Miller (wrote the screenplay for Marilyn Monroe in 1961).

3. *The Mayor of Casterbridge*, by Thomas Hardy (published in 1886).

4. Mao Zedong's wife, Jiang Qing (in 1964).

5. The Taj Mahal (built by Shah Jahan as a tomb for his wife, Mumtaz Mahal, beginning in 1632).

6. Jean-Louis Barrault (in 1947).

7. The hanging gardens of Babylon (*c*. 580 BC).

8. Stanley Spencer (in 1937).

9. Berkeley Castle (in 1327; he was imprisoned there by Queen Isabella and Roger Mortimer).

10. John Ruskin (Millais married Ruskin's wife, Effie, in 1855).

59 BRIDGES

1. The Sant'Angelo Bridge (built in about AD 105, leading to his mausoleum; now the Castel Sant'Angelo).

2. *A View from the Bridge* (1955).

3. Suspension bridges (completed in 1826).

4. Sydney Harbour Bridge (Sydney Opera House, opened in 1973, is the other).

5. The Battle of Stirling Bridge.

6. The Clifton Suspension Bridge (over the Avon near Bristol).

7. *The Bridge on the River Kwai* (Alec Guinness was the third).

8. The onset of the most recent ice age (which caused the Bering Land Bridge to form between the two land masses).

9. The Battle of Milvian Bridge (AD 312).

10. Staten Island (the bridge was completed in 1964).

60 TRADE AND ECONOMICS

1. In China (from about AD 910; Marco Polo marvelled at it four centuries later).

2. The Fuggers.

3. Enron (in 2001).

4. Venice (a privilege, granted in 1082, that applied to the whole Byzantine empire).

5. Petra (the tombs were carved in Roman times, from about AD 200).

6. John D. Rockefeller's Standard Oil Company (in 1911).

7. The Great Leap Forward.

8. Sweden (the Bank of Sweden was founded in 1668; the Bank of England followed in 1694).

9. The French fur trade (in 1608).

10. Investors or shareholders (the Act was passed in 1825).

61 JOSEPH

1. Joseph Paxton (in 1840, eleven years before his Crystal Palace was built).

2. Josephus (in AD 66).

3. Joseph Conrad (as a 21-year-old Polish citizen).

4. *The Selling of Joseph* (a very early anti-slavery tract, published in 1700).

5. Joseph Beuys (in 1965).

6. Melting ice (in 1761).

7. Pope Benedict XVI (elected in 2005).

8. Joseph Banks (he began collecting Pacific flora in 1769 with Daniel Solander and Herman Spöring).

9. Joseph Priestley (in 1774).

10. Joseph Bonaparte (transferred by his brother, Napoleon, in 1808).

62 BATTLES

1. Batalha, meaning 'battle' in Portuguese (the victory was over the king of Castile, in 1385).

2. The Battle of Dien Bien Phu (in Vietnam in 1954).

3. Robert the Bruce (king of the Scots, won at Bannockburn in 1314).

4. Claude Auchinleck (in 1942 – Montgomery drove Rommel back to the west in the second battle of El Alamein, later in the same year).

5. Simon de Montfort (in 1265; leading the English barons in rebellion, de Montfort had captured Henry III at Lewes in the previous year).

6. Vimy Ridge (taken in 1917).

7. Vercingetorix (he was subsequently taken to Rome to be displayed in Caesar's triumph and then killed).

8. Père Lachaise in Paris (the battle ended the Paris Commune, set up earlier in 1871 after the Franco-Prussian War).

9. At the river Boyne in Ireland (the Battle of the Boyne was conclusively won by William III in 1690).

10. It was the last sea battle to be fought between galleys propelled by oarsmen (Spanish and Venetian galleys defeated the Turks in 1571).

63 PAINTING

1. Lucas Cranach the Elder (from about 1525).

2. *The Mona Lisa* (Gherardini is the most probable candidate for Leonardo's sitter in this portrait, in about 1505).

3. Landscapes (often with cows), in the mid seventeenth century.

4. The Stanze (meaning simply 'rooms' in Italian; Raphael began work on them in 1509).

5. Greek vases (*c.* 550 BC).

6. Pointillism (though Seurat himself preferred the term Divisionism; from about 1885).

7. Romans living in Egypt (the portraits date from about AD 100).

8. International Gothic (*c.* 1400).

9. Graffiti (he died of an overdose in 1988).

10. Marcel Duchamp (in 1912).

64 STEPHEN

1. Matilda, also known as the empress Maud (he managed to retain the throne himself from 1135, but was succeeded on his death in 1154 by her son Henry II).

2. Stephen Spender (his poem 'The Pylons' was published in 1933).

3. *Duel* (1971).

4. Steve Davis (in 1981).

5. Abraham Lincoln (in the Lincoln–Douglas debates of 1858 on the issue of slavery).

6. *Billy Elliott* (2000).

7. 'John Brown's Body' (the book-length poem was published in 1928).

8. Texas (when it was still a province of Mexico, in 1821).

9. Steve Biko (in Pretoria, in 1977).

10. The Apple computer (designed and marketed in 1976 by Steve Wozniak and Steve Jobs).

65 SHIPS AND BOATS

1. A flying boat (in 1912).

2. The caravel (*c.* 1450).

3. Henley (in 1829).

4. Enrique Granados (in 1916).

5. It was high in the air, on a cast-iron aqueduct built by Thomas Telford (opened in 1805).

6. Sutton Hoo, in Suffolk (the Sutton Hoo Ship Burial, possibly of King Raedwald; the ship was buried in about AD 625 and excavated in 1939).

7. *Showboat* (the 1936 film of the Jerome Kern musical).

8. The *Kon-Tiki* (on which he crossed the Pacific from Peru in 1947).

9. She was a steamboat (launched in 1807).

10. 'Cargoes' (written by John Masefield in 1910).

66 ASTRONOMY AND SPACE

1. Pluto (in 2006).

2. Valentina Tereshkova (in 1963, in *Vostok* 6).

3. Georgium Sidus, or the Georgian Star (in honour of George III).

4. Anders Celsius (in 1742).

5. The successful docking in space of their US and Soviet spacecraft (*Apollo* and *Soyuz*) in 1975.

6. Our present Gregorian calendar (introduced by Pope Gregory XIII).

7. Asteroids (photographed in close-up by the US spacecraft *Galileo* in 1991).

8. Omar Khayyam (*c.* 1080; the verses are referred to collectively as his *Rubaiyat*, meaning 'quatrains').

9. The return of the comet now known by his name (in 1758, as he had predicted; he died in 1742).

10. Laika (the dog in *Sputnik II* in 1957).

67 BIRDS

1. John James Audubon (the volumes were completed in 1838).

2. Margaret Drabble (the book was published in 1963).

3. The *corvus*, or 'raven'.

4. Michel Fokine (in 1910).

5. Carrier pigeons, or homing pigeons (*c.* 1050).

6. Saxophonist Charlie Parker (from 1939).

7. Passenger pigeon (she died in 1914 at the age of twenty-nine).

8. Harper Lee (the novel was *To Kill a Mockingbird*).

9. *Birdsong* (1993).

10. Olivier Messiaen (in 1953).

68 TWO

1. Jean-Jacques Rousseau (in 1762, causing him to go into exile in Switzerland).

2. Doric and Ionic (*c.* 650 BC – followed by the Corinthian about 200 years later).

3. Charles V, the Holy Roman Emperor (in 1556).

4. Greta Garbo (in 1941).

5. Ostrogoths and Visigoths (*c.* AD 250).

6. Jeeves and Bertie Wooster (in the collection of stories with that title by P. G. Wodehouse, published in 1917).

7. Pheidippides (before the Battle of Marathon, in 490 BC).

8. Paris and London (in *A Tale of Two Cities*, published in 1859).

9. Henry David Thoreau (he published *Walden; or, Life in the Woods* in 1854).

10. *Persuasion* (both books were published in 1818).

69 CASTLE

1. Balmoral Castle (which they altered and enlarged until 1856).

2. Martin Luther's 95 Theses (which he nailed to the church door in 1517, virtually launching the Reformation).

3. Lord Castlereagh (Robert Stewart, 2nd Marquess of Londonderry, in 1809).

4. Richard II (who ceded the crown to Henry IV in 1399 and died in 1400).

5. Canossa (in 1077; the pope was Gregory VII).

6. Robert Lowell (the collection was published in 1946).

7. Edinburgh Castle (designed by Robert Lorimer and unveiled in 1927).

8. The Alhambra (begun in 1238).

9. The Habsburg dynasty (the castle was built in about 1020).

10. *Axel's Castle* (1931).

70 NEW YORK

1. Alfred Stieglitz and Edward Steichen (in 1905).

2. For a headquarters for the new United Nations (in 1946).

3. Henry Hudson, after whom the river is named (in 1609).

4. Diedrich Knickerbocker, used as a pen-name by Washington Irving (the book was published in 1809).

5. By cutting the rope from which the platform he was standing on was suspended (the platform remained firmly in place).

6. *The Bonfire of the Vanities* (1987).

7. A crossword (devised by English-born journalist Arthur Wynne).

8. California (in 1958).

9. *Guys and Dolls* (1932).

10. The Armory Show (held in 1913 in New York City's 69th Regiment Armory on Lexington Avenue).

71 WAR

1. Constantinople (the bombardment led to the fall of the city).

2. By breaching their own dikes (and thus threatening the Spanish troops outside the town with death by drowning, in 1573).

3. Tommy Sopwith (his company was founded in 1912 to manufacture planes, and produced these models for military purposes).

4. The soldiers themselves, a very effective new social and military convention (from about 550 BC).

5. Germany (the Messerschmitt Me 262, in 1944).

6. Three (the first Afghan War, 1839–42, the Second Afghan War, 1878–81, and the Third Afghan War, 1919–21).

7. The Battle of Midway (in 1942).

8. Against the British (the War of 1812, which lasted until 1815).

9. The 38th parallel north (the war lasted from 1950 to 1953).

10. No change (the war, launched by Iraq in 1980, lasted until 1988).

72 FILM

1. It was the first film with a soundtrack (in this case, a synchronized musical score; the first 'talkies' followed a year later, in 1927).

2. Pablo Neruda (in the Oscar-winning film of 1994).

3. *The Battleship Potemkin* (1925).

4. *The Silence of the Lambs* (1991).

5. Satyajit Ray (in 1955).

6. *Buena Vista Social Club* (a documentary by Wim Wenders, released in 1999).

7. *Raise the Red Lantern* (1991).

8. *What's New Pussycat?* (1965).

9. *Henry V* (1944 – Walton also wrote the score for Olivier's *Richard III* in 1955).

10. *The Wizard of Oz* (directed by Victor Fleming).

73 FELINES

1. Bagheera (in Rudyard Kipling's *Jungle Book*, published in 1894).

2. Ang Lee (in 2000).

3. Tamil Tigers (LTTE stands for Liberation Tigers of Tamil Eelam, who launched an ongoing civil war in 1983).

4. Ashurbanipal (*c.* 645 BC; the relief is now in the British Museum).

5. The Lions (from 1924).

6. William I, or William the Lion (in 1174).

7. Etruscan culture (*c.* 550 BC).

8. The Open Championship (or British Open) and the US Masters (in 1997).

9. Ancient Egypt (from about 2500 BC – and they were much mummified).

10. *The Lion, the Witch and the Wardrobe* (1950).

74 FIRE

1. *Henry VIII* (in 1613).

2. Savonarola (in the carnival before Lent in 1497).

3. Harvey Firestone (the Firestone Tire and Rubber Company was established in 1900).

4. *Pale Fire* (1962).

5. Vesta (the Vestal Virgins, from about 300 BC).

6. The Spitfire (in 1936).

7. *Chariots of Fire* (directed by Hugh Hudson).

8. 'Keep the Home Fires Burning' (1914).

9. 'Fireside chats' (from 1933).

10. San Francisco.

75 CONFINEMENT

1. Robben Island, in Table Bay (Mandela was sentenced to life imprisonment in 1964).

2. Boethius (*c.* 525).

3. The piece consists of 4 minutes and 33 seconds of silence.

4. Marco Polo (in 1298).

5. Newgate Gaol (in 1868).

6. Ethel Smyth (in 1912).

7. On a prison ship (his poem of 1781, *The British Prison Ship*, was an account of his unpleasant experiences in British hands).

8. Elizabeth Fry (from about 1813).

9. Dietrich Bonhoeffer (in 1944).

10. Thomas Paine (in 1793).

76 AUSTRALIA

1. George Bass (in 1798).

2. Canberra (an entirely new capital for Australia; the Australian parliament moved there from Melbourne in 1927).

3. Ayers Rock (in 1985).

4. Vegemite.

5. The White Australia policy (the pamphlet was published in 1960).

6. *The Fatal Shore* (1987).

7. The Holden (prime minister Ben Chifley witnessed the completion of the first official example).

8. Nellie Melba (Pêche Melba was created in about 1892).

9. Harold Holt (near Portsea, south of Melbourne, in 1967).

10. As an Aboriginal artist (the first exhibition of his watercolours was in 1938).

77 COURTS

1. Jahangir (in 1615).

2. Richard Nixon (when they were taking the first steps towards impeaching him).

3. Slavery (a judgment on the legal status of slaves, in 1857).

4. Augusto Pinochet (who returned to Chile rather than being extradited to Spain in 2000).

5. Alfred Dreyfus (in 1898).

6. Mae West (in 1927).

7. He was the first African-American member of the US Supreme Court (appointed by Lyndon Johnson in 1967).

8. John Ashbery (in 1962).

9. Cicero.

10. The right to a minimum wage (in 1907).

78 THREE

1. Muhammad Ali (in 1964, 1974 and 1978).

2. Karl Friedrich Benz (in 1885).

3. Betty Cuthbert (for the 100m, 200m and 400m).

4. Frederick II of Prussia, or Frederick the Great (his victories were won in 1745 against the Austrians in the War of the Austrian Succession).

5. Alvar Aalto (in 1938).

6. Manuel de Falla (for the Ballets Russes in 1917).

7. China (construction began in 1993 and was completed in 2006).

8. *Henry VI* (1591–2).

9. Paestum (the earliest of the three was built in about 530 BC).

10. Helen Clark (in 2005).

79 BLACK

1. Their black shirts (an Italian Fascist uniform, in 1922).

2. Charles Dickens (in 1824).

3. The British Museum (in *Blackmail*, 1929).

4. Walter Blackie (the house was commissioned in 1902 and completed in 1904).

5. Black holes (as first described by British physicist Stephen Hawking in 1974).

6. *The Souls of Black Folk* (1903).

7. The blacksmith ('The Village Blacksmith' was published in 1841).

8. The Black Death (in 1347).

9. *The Harmonious Blacksmith* (published by Handel in 1720, and the theme and variations by Percy Grainger in 1930).

10. The Black Hole of Calcutta.

80 THE PACIFIC

1. Alexander Selkirk (rescued in 1709; Daniel Defoe's *Robinson Crusoe* was published in 1719).

2. The Greenpeace ship *Rainbow Warrior* (in 1985).

3. Hawaii (also known as Big Island, the largest of the islands in the Hawaiian Archipelago, in 1779).

4. The hydrogen bomb (tested by the US in 1951).

5. The Aloha Concert (in 1973).

6. Iwo Jima (in 1945).

7. Ferdinand Magellan (landed in Guam in 1521).

8. Samoa (in *Coming of Age in Samoa*, published in 1928).

9. The Hawaiian Islands (in 1898).

10. Paul Gauguin.

81 CANADA

1. Canada's centennial celebration in 1967 (the independent Dominion of Canada was established in 1867).

2. Greenpeace.

3. Lord Durham (it is often referred to as Lord Durham's Report).

4. The Assembly of First Nations (AFN, set up in 1982).

5. The Arctic (he went up through the Great Slave Lake to reach the Arctic Ocean in 1789).

6. Robertson Davies (he completed the series in 1975).

7. Mikhail Baryshnikov (in 1974).

8. Marshall McLuhan (the book was published in 1962).

9. John Cabot (exploring on behalf of the English king, Henry VII, in 1497).

10. The Great Lakes (by the opening of the St Lawrence Seaway in 1959).

1. The Shi'a Party (the schism was over the issue of succession after the death in AD 661 of Muhammad's son-in-law, the fourth caliph, Ali).

2. The Communist League, or Communists (in 1847).

3. The African National Congress (ANC).

4. The Ba'th Party (founded in about 1943, subsequently establishing dictatorships in both Syria and Iraq).

5. The Guomindang, or Nationalist Party (in 1910).

6. The National Socialist German Workers' Party, shortened to the Nazi Party (in 1920; Adolf Hitler was already a leading member).

7. J. M. Hertzog, to represent Afrikaner interests (in 1914).

8. The Bull Moose Party (so called after a reporter asked Roosevelt about his health during the campaign and he replied that he felt like a bull moose, in 1912).

9. The Carbonari (first appeared in 1806).

10. The Federalists following Hamilton and the Republicans supporting Jefferson (from 1792).

83 ISLANDS

1. Torcello (*c.* AD 820).

2. Hong Kong (ceded by China in the Treaty of Nanking in 1842).

3. The Gambia.

4. Elba (he was sent to St Helena in 1815).

5. Crete (Knossos was an important centre in Minoan Crete, in about 2000 BC).

6. Uraniborg (built in about 1576).

7. Las Islas Malvinas (in 1774).

8. Macau (in 1999; the Portuguese had signed a treaty with imperial China in 1887 giving them 'perpetual occupation and government' of the island).

9. France (it is in French Guiana; Alfred Dreyfus was sent there in 1894).

10. Barra (the Ealing comedy was filmed in 1949).

84 BOOK

1. *The Tale of Genji* (completed in 1001).

2. Jews, Christians and Muslims.

3. Cricket (spelt 'creckett', describing the game as played in a Guildford school in 1598).

4. Johann Sebastian Bach (in 1720).

5. Ireland (*c.* AD 650).

6. Vitruvius (*De Architectura*, written in about 20 BC).

7. Jean Fouquet (in 1452).

8. The Baedeker *Tourist Guide to Britain* (the 'Baedeker raids' of 1942 were against historic British cities with three stars in the book).

9. The *Domesday Book* (a survey of land-holdings in Norman England for taxation purposes, undertaken in 1086 and completed in 1087).

10. The 'Book of the Dead' (*c.* 1550 BC).

85 ENGLAND

1. The Jews (banned from residence by a law passed in 1290, they returned from about 1656 with Cromwell's approval).

2. Samuel Richardson (his *Clarissa* was published in seven volumes in 1747–8).

3. The *Rocket* (the locomotive built by George and Robert Stephenson, in the 1829 trials at Rainhill, near Liverpool).

4. Capability Brown, or Lancelot Brown (he set up in business as a freelance landscape consultant in 1751).

5. John Nash (in 1815).

6. Henry King (who died in a shipwreck in 1637; the poem was published in 1638).

7. Stockings (the device, invented by William Lee in 1589, may be the world's first example of industrial machinery).

8. The smoking of tobacco (in *A Counterblast to Tobacco*, published in 1604).

9. London and Bristol (from 1784, greatly speeding up communication).

10. The Crystal Palace (built in 1851 for the Great Exhibition).

86 GOLD

1. *She Stoops to Conquer* (in the Covent Garden Theatre).

2. Kyoto (in 1397).

3. Henry James (the book was published in 1904).

4. Brazil.

5. From the name of the young harpsichordist (Johann Gottlieb Goldberg) for whom the variations are traditionally believed to have been written.

6. The Eureka Stockade (the diggers were protesting against compulsory licensing).

7. Le Corbusier (the Modulor was introduced in 1940).

8. Henry VIII and Francis I, the kings of England and France (in 1520).

9. The gold standard (formally adopted in 1819, though it had been used on a de facto basis since 1717, and finally abandoned in 1931).

10. Nikolai Rimsky-Korsakov.

87 GEORGE

1. George (Gilbert & George, or Gilbert Prousch and George Passmore, first became well known in 1969 as performance artists).

2. George Vancouver (sailed in 1791 and reached the regions now known as Vancouver and Vancouver Island in the following year).

3. George Sand (she met him in 1836).

4. George Boole (Boolean algebra; the pamphlet was published in 1847).

5. Georgia, in the USA (granted by George II).

6. George Marshall (the Marshall Plan provided US aid to rebuild Europe).

7. George Berkeley (subsequently often known as Bishop Berkeley; his book was published in 1710).

8. George Gallup (the Institute was founded in 1935 and pioneered modern polling techniques).

9. George Formby (the first record was released in 1929).

10. George Westinghouse (in 1893).

88 CITIES

1. Constantinople (created by the emperor Constantine on the site of ancient Byzantium).

2. Karakorum (developed in about 1230).

3. Hamburg (the word in German is '*Feuersturm*').

4. *The City of God* (*c.* AD 413).

5. *City Lights* (1931).

6. Antioch (now Antakya, in 1098).

7. Isfahan (from 1598).

8. Mahagonny (the opera, *Rise and Fall of the City of Mahagonny*, opened in Leipzig in 1930).

9. Moscow (in 1812).

10. A theatrical contest, with competitions for the best comedy and tragedy.

89 GREECE

1. The emperor Nero (in AD 66).

2. The one-eyed Cyclopes (the style of architecture is known as Cyclopean).

3. The ancient games at Olympia (forbidden from 393 by the Roman emperor Theodosius).

4. Stars (Hipparchus completed his catalogue in 129 BC).

5. Bavaria (Otto, Prince of Bavaria, became King Otto of Greece in 1832).

6. Socrates (*Clouds* was performed in Athens in 423 BC).

7. Maria Callas.

8. For the Parthenon (building began in Athens in 447 BC and continued for ten years).

9. Aristotle (tutor to Alexander, subsequently Alexander the Great, from 343 BC).

10. Britain (Lord Palmerston sent a naval squadron in 1850 to seize Greek ships, because Don Pacifico was a British subject).

90 PETER

1. Peter Abelard's (because of his affair with one of his pupils, Héloïse).

2. The Olympic games (he organized the first modern Olympics, in Athens in 1896).

3. The Pierrot Players (they were formed in 1967 and became The Fires of London in 1970).

4. In St Peter's in Rome (Charlemagne was crowned emperor by Pope Leo III; Charlemagne maintained that he didn't know it was going to happen).

5. Pierre Trudeau.

6. Peter Carey (the book was published in 1985).

7. Joseph Haydn (in 1790; during that decade Salomon presented Haydn's twelve London symphonies).

8. Peter Stuyvesant (in office from 1647 until 1664, when he ceded the territory, including Manhattan, to the English).

9. Musique concrète (in 1948).

10. *Stolen Generations* (1981).

91 FLIGHT

1. Insects (*c.* 360 million years ago).

2. *Spirit of St Louis* (in 1927).

3. Gothic (they are skeletal buttresses, as strong as solid ones but much lighter).

4. A glider (from 1891, launching from a hill near Potsdam).

5. Louis Blériot (in 1909).

6. John Alcock and Arthur Whitten Brown (after making the first transatlantic flight, from Newfoundland).

7. Salvador Dalí (in 1951; the painting is now in Kelvingrove Art Gallery, Glasgow).

8. Orville Wright (on the toss of a coin – his brother Wilbur, flying next, travelled nearly sixty yards on the same morning of 17 December 1903).

9. *Monty Python's Flying Circus.*

10. Charles Stewart Rolls (in 1910).

92 NEWS

1. *Il Risorgimento* (meaning 'the resurgence').

2. Annie Proulx (the book was published in 1993).

3. *The New Yorker* (he founded it in 1925 and remained in charge until his death in 1951).

4. Alexander Herzen (in 1857).

5. 'All the news that's fit to print.'

6. The Cherokee (in 1828).

7. The discovery of gold (sparking the great California Gold Rush in 1848).

8. John Tenniel (who first drew for *Punch* in 1850).

9. *Pravda* (first published in 1912; the name means 'truth' in Russian).

10. The *Tatler* (launched in 1709 – the *Spectator* followed in 1711).

93 THE INDIAN SUBCONTINENT

1. After the Indian Mutiny, or First War of Indian Independence (in 1858).

2. Gandhara (the style of sculpture developed from about AD 100).

3. Robert Clive (in 1751).

4. Edwin Lutyens (construction began in New Delhi in 1913).

5. Sirimavo Bandaranaike (widow of Solomon Bandaranaike; she served as prime minister of Sri Lanka in 1960–65, 1970–77 and 1994–2000).

6. The British tax on salt (in 1930).

7. Mujibur Rahman (arrested in 1971; he subsequently became the first prime minister of Bangladesh in 1972).

8. The *Ramayana* (probably the work of a single author in about 300 BC).

9. Mother Teresa (in Calcutta, in 1952).

10. Nadir Shah (taking among other things the famous Peacock Throne of Shah Jahan, in 1739).

94 SLAVERY

1. *Uncle Tom's Cabin* (published in 1852; it sold 300,000 copies in its first year).

2. 1807 (in both cases the slave trade was made illegal, but not slavery).

3. The Cape Verde islands (in 1466).

4. The Republican Party (formed in 1854, the origin of the present-day Republican Party).

5. David Livingstone (Blantyre in Scotland was his birthplace, in 1813).

6. The balance between 'free' and 'slave' states in the US Senate ('free' Maine and 'slave' Missouri were admitted respectively in 1820 and 1821).

7. The Code of Hammurabi (*c.* 1800 BC; it is the earliest surviving document to mention laws relating to slaves).

8. The right to reclaim even those slaves who had escaped to the anti-slavery 'free' states in the North.

9. Jamaica (settled by the British from 1655).

10. The Thirteenth Amendment (passed in 1865).

95 NEWLY

1. Ignacy Jan Paderewski.

2. George Bernard Shaw (in 1884).

3. 'Mary had a little lamb' (in 1877).

4. Jefferson Davis (in 1861, at first only provisionally).

5. Las Malvinas, known as the Falklands to the British (in 1820).

6. Lech Walesa (in 1980).

7. Intel (in 1969).

8. Graham Sutherland.

9. Walter Gropius (in 1919).

10. Gian Lorenzo Bernini (in 1629).

96 FICTION

1. The events described in both take place within a single day (*Ulysses* was published in 1922 and *Mrs Dalloway* in 1925).

2. Natty Bumppo, the hero of all Cooper's 'Leatherstocking Tales' (*The Last of the Mohicans* was published in 1826).

3. Rugby (Thomas Hughes's novel *Tom Brown's Schooldays* was published in 1857).

4. Quasimodo (in Victor Hugo's *The Hunchback of Notre-Dame*, published in 1831).

5. A giant peach (in *James and the Giant Peach*).

6. *On the Road* (1957).

7. The Glass family, created by J. D. Salinger (*Franny and Zooey*, published in 1961, was his second volume of stories about the family).

8. Sir Percy Blakeney (who rescued French aristocrats from the guillotine in Baroness Orczy's *The Scarlet Pimpernel*, published in 1905).

9. The Roman emperor Claudius (Claudius died in AD 54; *I, Claudius* was published in 1934).

10. Pollyanna, or Polyanna Whittier (*Pollyanna* was published in 1913 and was followed by numerous spin-offs throughout the century).

97 FIVE

1. Non-Conformist ministers in England (the Act of 1665 prevented them from going within five miles of any town where they had ministered).

2. The 1920s (the Plan was adopted in 1929, aiming for a massive increase in agricultural and industrial output but resulting in an actual decline).

3. The Homestead Act (passed in 1862).

4. The Dionne family (the famous Dionne Quintuplets were born in 1934 in Corbeil, Ontario).

5. In the House of Commons in London (when Charles I arrived to arrest them in 1642).

6. The Famous Five (who appeared for the first time in *Five on a Treasure Island*).

7. Mr Five Percent (5 per cent was his cut on each deal).

8. Sikhism (the Kesh, Kangha, Kachha, Kara and Kirpan, introduced by the guru Gobind Rai in 1699).

9. The Olympic Games (held at Olympia since 776 BC, the traditional founding date).

10. The first safety elevator (installed in 1857, which made possible the future development of skyscrapers).

98 FORD OR BRIDGE

1. Cambridge (in 1636; it acquired its present name when John Harvard gave it a large bequest, in 1638).

2. William Bradford, who was the governor of New Plymouth from 1621 (he began his journal in 1620; it was published in 1856).

3. Ironbridge (the world's first cast-iron bridge, crossing the Severn, was erected in 1779).

4. Ernest Rutherford (in 1903).

5. Casterbridge (in Thomas Hardy's novel *The Mayor of Casterbridge*, published in 1886).

6. Francis Ford Coppola (the film was released in 1979).

7. Bridget Riley (from 1960).

8. The Battle of Stamford Bridge (he defeated the Norwegian king Harald Hardraade in September, three weeks before his death at Hastings).

9. Oxford (it was subsequently known as the *Oxford English Dictionary*).

10. Stanford University (they registered www.google.com in 1997).

99 PAUL

1. Paul Newman (in 1958).

2. The *Raj Quartet* (of which *The Jewel in the Crown* was the first volume, published in 1966).

3. Paul Verlaine (in 1870).

4. V. S. Naipaul's family (in his 1961 novel).

5. Paul von Hindenburg (in 1934).

6. The Peter and Paul Fortress (captured in 1917).

7. St Luke (the Acts were written in about AD 75).

8. Paul Hindemith (in 1934).

9. Wolfgang Pauli (in 1930).

10. Paul Whiteman (in 1926).

1. Alexander Jean Fresnel (published the theory in 1821; his lens, designed for lighthouses, was first put into use in 1822).

2. The first Soviet atomic bomb ('Joe' referred to Joseph Stalin).

3. Isaac Newton (experimenting with the prism in 1672).

4. William Gilbert (in 1600).

5. They were the first to split an atom (in 1932).

6. Hans Geiger (he developed the Geiger counter in 1908).

7. Enrico Fermi (in 1942).

8. Albert Einstein (in 1939).

9. Alessandro Volta (in 1800).

10. Uranium (in 1896).

101 MUSIC, PATRIOTIC AND POPULAR

1. 'America' (in 1831).

2. The Beach Boys (in 1973).

3. Edith Piaf (from '*la môme piaf*', 'the little sparrow', from 1935).

4. London and Philadelphia (in 1985).

5. 'The Marseillaise' (in 1792).

6. Bessie Smith (in 1923).

7. Lil Hardin Armstrong, the wife of Louis Armstrong (in 1925).

8. Cliff Richard (in 1958; followed by hits through six decades into the new millennium).

9. Boogie-woogie (the record was 'Pinetop's Boogie-Woogie', issued in 1928).

10. 'Yankee Doodle' (from 1775).

102 PARIS

1. Picasso's *Guernica* (in 1937).

2. The Gobelin family (in 1662).

3. Josephine Baker (in 1925).

4. *Hernani* (in 1830).

5. The Pompidou Centre (opened in 1977).

6. *Sous les toits de Paris* (1930).

7. The Pont Neuf (in 1985).

8. The rotation of the earth (proved by the motion of the pendulum that he suspended from the dome of the Panthéon in 1851).

9. The Statue of Liberty (in 1885).

10. Art Deco (from the Exposition Internationale des Arts Décoratifs, Industriels et Modernes in 1925).

103 DICTATORS

1. Tikrit, the town of his birth (the farm where he was found, in 2003, is part of a small agricultural town, ad-Dawr).

2. In Rome (in 1347).

3. His son Kim Jong Il (in 1994).

4. Peisistratus (in 560 BC).

5. Manuel Noriega (in 1990).

6. The Dominican Republic (in 1930).

7. Rwanda.

8. Achmed Sukarno (in 1959).

9. *The Great Dictator* (1940).

10. Simón Bolívar (in 1823).

104 DISCOVERIES

1. The *Discovery* (sailed from the UK in 1901).

2. Silver (rich seams were discovered in 1545).

3. In the Neander Valley, near Düsseldorf (in 1856; '*Neanderthal*' is German for 'Neander valley').

4. Bakelite.

5. Oil (he formed the Burman Oil Company).

6. The ozone layer, in the stratosphere (in 1913).

7. John Hanning Speke (in 1858).

8. Porcelain (the technique had been known for centuries in China but remained a mystery in Europe until Böttger's discovery in 1708).

9. St James (the remains were discovered in about AD 825 – and eventually the place became known as Santiago de Compostela).

10. That it has a mathematical basis (in about 500 BC, they discovered that the ratio between the highest and lowest pitch of an octave is 2:1).

105 COURTS

1. Oxford (from 1642).

2. Francisco de Goya (in 1789).

3. Joseph II (in Vienna in 1790).

4. Nefertiti (wife of the pharaoh Akhenaten; the sculpture was made in about 1340 BC).

5. Nepal (in 2001).

6. Hampton Court (given to Henry VIII in an attempt to remain in favour in 1528).

7. Munich (in 1865).

8. Titian (in 1533).

9. Anthony van Dyck (in 1632).

10. The Hermitage (in St Petersburg, founded in 1764).

106 SOUTHERN AFRICA

1. Mahatma Gandhi (because of his colour, in 1893).

2. Trekboers (from about 1775).

3. The Zulu (from 1816).

4. The Congress of Vienna (in 1815).

5. Angola (the war ended with the disbanding of UNITA in 2002).

6. Cape Town (established in 1652).

7. Bartolomeu Dias (sailing for the king of Portugal, in 1488).

8. Nelson Mandela and F. W. de Klerk (in 1993).

9. Afrikaners (eager to see themselves as African rather than Dutch, in about 1795).

10. Joshua Nkomo (leader of the Zimbabwe African People's Union, defeated in the election of 1980).

107 TRADE AND ECONOMICS

1. Friedrich Engels (in 1842 – his experiences led him to publish *The Condition of the Working Class in England* in 1845).

2. Coco Chanel (opened her shop in 1912; introduced Chanel No. 5 in 1922).

3. Spanish galleons (Portobelo is a port town in Panama, from which the mineral treasures of America were shipped back to Spain from about 1550).

4. Twelve (in 1802).

5. Palmyra (from about 200 BC).

6. Saltaire (built in 1851, on the banks of the River Aire in Yorkshire).

7. Alaska (in 1799).

8. Cigarettes (in 1884).

9. Across Panama, in the region most suitable for a canal (full sovereignty over the canal region was restored to Panama in 1999).

10. The Phoenicians (from about 950 BC, during the reign of Hiram of Tyre, who traded with the Israelite king Solomon).

108 THE CARIBBEAN

1. The Wailers (formed in Kingston, Jamaica, in 1963).

2. Trinidadian cricketer Brian Lara (in 1994; he beat by two runs the previous world record of 499 runs scored by Hanif Mohammad in 1959).

3. Jamaica Kincaid (the novel was published in 1985).

4. Havana (in 1898).

5. Jean-Bertrand Aristide (fled in 1991, returned under UN protection in 1994 and fled again in 2004).

6. The Rough Riders (in 1898).

7. Derek Walcott (he founded the theatre company in 1959 and won the Nobel Prize for Literature in 1992).

8. Guantanamo Bay (from 1903).

9. Jamaica (*c.* 1930).

10. François ('Papa Doc') Duvalier (president of Haiti from 1964).

109 MEDICINE

1. Anaesthetic (in 1847; he used ether and then chloroform later in the same year).

2. Exposure to x-rays (discovered in 1903).

3. Harold Gillies (the book was published in 1920; he had set up a plastic surgery unit in Britain in 1916).

4. 'Test tube baby' (she was born in 1978 after being conceived by in vitro fertilization).

5. Leonardo da Vinci (*c.* 1489).

6. The collective unconscious (introduced as such in 1912; Jung later preferred to call it the objective psyche).

7. Alois Alzheimer (identified in 1906, as a physical condition, the disease now known as Alzheimer's).

8. Plastic surgery (Susruta, working in about 550 BC, specialized in repairing damage to the nose).

9. Smoking and lung cancer (the report, by Austin Hill and Richard Doll, was published in 1950).

10. Ambroise Paré.

110 LOVE

1. The British king Edward VIII (subsequently Duke of Windsor; he abdicated in 1936 to marry the love of his life, American divorcée Wallis Simpson).

2. Gabriel García Márquez (the book was published in 1985).

3. Petrarch (in 1327, or so he tells us).

4. Harry Lauder (in 1907).

5. Pablo Neruda (the collection was published in 1924).

6. The bomb (*Dr Strangelove, or: How I Learned to Stop Worrying and Love the Bomb* was released in 1964).

7. Anna Karenina (in Tolstoy's novel of that title, published in 1875).

8. Ovid (in about 20 BC).

9. James Woodforde (*The Diary of a Country Parson* ran from 1758 to 1802).

10. Oliver Mellors (the gamekeeper in D. H. Lawrence's novel *Lady Chatterley's Lover*, published in 1928).

111 FIRSTS

1. Sanskrit (it is a collection of sacrificial hymns of the Aryans, dating from about 1500 BC).

2. Christiaan Barnard (performed the first heart transplant in 1967).

3. Sikhism (in the Punjab around 1500).

4. Tabriz (*c.* 1300).

5. *Ab Urbe Condita* ('from the founding of the city'; 753 BC is traditionally Rome's first year).

6. Beatrix Potter herself (in 1901).

7. She was the first female bishop (in the Anglican Communion's line of succession from St Peter).

8. Buddhism (the book is *The Diamond Sutra*, printed in AD 868).

9. *Anne of Green Gables* (1908).

10. Gunpowder.

112 METAL

1. Korea (in about 1300 – the Chinese had attempted to make movable type before then, using fired clay, but it proved impractical).

2. Henry Cort (in 1784).

3. Daibutsu (literally 'great Buddha', cast in 1252).

4. Anthony Caro (from 1960).

5. Brass (melted down from objects brought in by traders from about 1500).

6. *The Tin Drum* (1959).

7. Mildenhall, in Suffolk (the Mildenhall Treasure is now in the British Museum).

8. Trinidad (*c.* 1930).

9. Russian guns captured in the Crimean War (in 1857).

10. Copper-plate writing (the first book of examples was published by Gianfrancesco Cresci in 1560).

113 ISLANDS

1. Bombay, or Mumbai.

2. Rhodes (from 1309 – they moved to Malta in 1530).

3. Anatole France (the book was published in 1908).

4. Samuel Johnson and James Boswell (in 1773).

5. Milos, or Milo (the Aphrodite of Milos, better known as the Venus de Milo, dates from about 100 BC).

6. Rhode Island (in 1636).

7. The Spice Islands (because of the trade in cloves, originally Portuguese but forcibly taken over by the Dutch from about 1625).

8. The lighthouse at Alexandria, one of the Seven Wonders of the World (built in about 280 BC).

9. Jacques Cartier (in 1535).

10. The Statue of Liberty (erected in New York Bay on Bedloe's Island, also known as Liberty Island, in 1886).

114 NEW

1. At Jamestown, Virginia (in 1607).

2. Homeopathy (from the Greek for 'like suffering', because the treatment of a complaint administered tiny doses of a drug expected in larger quantities to provoke similar symptoms).

3. A new calendar, the Julian calendar (introduced in 45 BC, by which time the existing system was three months out of step with the seasons).

4. *Aida* (first performed in 1871).

5. 'Waltzing Matilda' (in Australia).

6. Geoffrey Chaucer.

7. Temple Mount in Jerusalem (construction began in 20 BC).

8. Charles Barry (work began in 1837 – the interiors were designed by Augustus Welby Pugin).

9. Louis Botha (in 1910).

10. Joseph Bazalgette (in 1859).

115 BRITAIN

1. Edward Heath (in 1973; the Community became the European Union in 1993).

2. The Humber Bridge in Britain (at 1410 metres, it was the longest in the world from 1981 until 1998, when the 1991m Akashi-Kaikyo Bridge in Japan was opened).

3. Canary Wharf (in 1996).

4. Spencer Perceval (killed in the lobby of the House of Commons by John Bellingham in 1812).

5. The Spice Girls (the album was *Spice*).

6. Belgrade (in 1958; after take-off from Belgrade the plane had stopped in Munich to refuel).

7. A poll tax (of one shilling a head; provoking the revolt of 1381 in Essex and Kent).

8. Bread and potatoes.

9. The Samaritans (began their work with the depressed and suicidal in 1953).

10. *War Requiem* (in 1962).

116 ENGINEERING

1. Tower Bridge (a bascule bridge raises its roadway to let ships pass through).

2. Concorde (1969 was the year in which it made its first supersonic test flight).

3. Wood (the Mosquito was an all-purpose military plane designed by de Havilland and manufactured from 1941).

4. The helicopter (in 1939; he used a rotor on a long tail boom to counter torque).

5. The first tunnel under the Thames (Marc Isambard Brunel and Isambard Kingdom Brunel completed it in 1843).

6. Wernher von Braun (appointed in 1937; he was taken to the USA in 1945 to head the US intercontinental ballistic missile programme).

7. A rotary engine (the model was made in 1924 and the prototype manufactured in 1954).

8. The Boulder Dam, or Hoover Dam (completed in 1935 and renamed the Hoover Dam in 1947).

9. The Firth of Forth, in Scotland (the bridge opened for trains in 1890).

10. Sergey Ilyushin (he began his career in 1926; the enterprise that he launched has manufactured planes ever since).

117 MISSIONS AND CRUSADES

1. President George W. Bush (in 2001).

2. 'Mission Accomplished' (seen behind President Bush as he delivered a televised speech from USS *Abraham Lincoln*, off the coast of California, three weeks after the fall of Baghdad in the Iraq War).

3. The Fourth Crusade (by crusaders transported to and from the sacked city of Constantinople in Venetian ships, in 1205).

4. Francis Xavier (in 1542).

5. A joint pact in defence of Poland (instead, in the Ribbentrop–Molotov pact, also in 1939, Russia and Germany agreed to divide Poland between them).

6. The Albigensian Crusade (against the Cathars, in 1208).

7. Torquato Tasso (the poem was completed in 1581).

8. They were Jesuits (the first of them arrived with Campion in 1580).

9. To lead an expedition up the Nile to rescue General Gordon, besieged with his garrison in Khartoum (in 1884).

10. The Children's Crusade (in 1212; a boy's visions of Jesus led thousands of young people to believe they could walk to the Holy Land to liberate it).

118 FOUR

1. *Eminent Victorians* (1918).

2. Donald Budge (in 1938).

3. The *Lusitania* (from 1907).

4. As the Year of the Four Emperors (Galba, Otho, Vitellius and Vespasian were successively proclaimed emperor in this chaotic year).

5. In T. S. Eliot's *Four Quartets* ('Burnt Norton', 'East Coker', 'The Dry Salvages' and 'Little Gidding', first published as a group in 1944).

6. *Duck Soup* (made in 1933, after which Zeppo withdrew).

7. His 'four freedoms', defined as necessities in any just society (freedom of speech, of worship, from want, from fear).

8. *An American in Paris* (composed by George Gershwin in 1928).

9. They were the dreaded Gang of Four, who held power in China from 1969 to 1976 (Yao Wenyan, Jiang Qing, Zhang Chungkiao and Wang Hongwen).

10. Walter Hagen (in 1922, 1924, 1928 and 1929).

119 BLACK AND WHITE

1. Tan (the Black and Tans were the brutal reinforcements for the British police in 1920).

2. Panther (the Black Panther Party was founded in 1966).

3. Blue (the Penny Black and Two Pence Blue, the world's first postage stamps, were both issued in 1840).

4. Blue (blue and white delftware, imitating the Chinese ceramic style, was available from about 1620).

5. Grey (in Whistler's painting of his mother entitled *Arrangement in Grey and Black*, 1871).

6. Red (in the first battle in the Wars of the Roses, between the white and red roses of York and Lancaster, in 1455).

7. Uruguay (in the civil war which began in 1838).

8. White (he painted his *White on White* series from 1918).

9. Grey (*Black Lamb and Grey Falcon* was published in 1941).

10. In the White House (he built the first Oval Office, in the new west wing, in 1909).

1. Egon Schiele (in 1912).

2. Éamon de Valéra (in 1919).

3. The Russian emperor Peter I, or Peter the Great (Alexis died in 1718).

4. Rudolf Hess (imprisoned with Hitler after the failed Munich Putsch in 1923).

5. Reading Gaol (in 1895, after he was convicted of homosexuality).

6. The French emperor Napoleon III (in 1870).

7. Belgium (in 1873; the incident happened in Brussels).

8. Winslow Homer (it was painted in 1866).

9. Richard I (returning from the Third Crusade in 1192).

10. The Bastille (in 1789).

121 RECORDS

1. *Anna Christie* (in 1931).

2. Malcolm Campbell (in 1939).

3. The Chrysler Building (in 1930; it lost the record in 1931 to the Empire State Building).

4. W. G. Grace (in 1876; his record was unbroken for the next forty-five years).

5. The baseball star Babe Ruth (in 1916).

6. Steam (later in the same year, William K. Vanderbilt added an extra 1 mph in the first internal-combustion car to set the record).

7. Francis Chichester (sailed solo round the world in record time, taking 226 days to return to Britain).

8. Howard Hughes (in 1935).

9. Britney Spears (with *In the Zone* in 2003).

10. Bob Beamon (jumped 8.9 metres in 1968 – his record was unsurpassed until Mike Powell achieved 8.95 metres in 1991).

122 THREE

1. Three Mile Island (in 1979).

2. Perkin Warbeck (hanged in 1499).

3. Johnny Weissmuller.

4. *A Fistful of Dollars* (1964).

5. The three Brontë sisters, Charlotte, Emily and Anne (the failure was followed, only a year later, by the sensationally successful publication of their first novels).

6. Francis Bacon (in 1945; the painting is now in the Tate).

7. The three-field system.

8. Fred Perry (his first win was in 1934).

9. Saul, the king of Israel (fighting against the Philistines in about 1000 BC).

10. The Short Parliament (dismissed in 1640 because it denied the king's request for funds).

123 WALES

1. The sixteenth century (under Henry VIII, in 1536).

2. Dylan Thomas (*Under Milk Wood* was broadcast on BBC radio in 1954).

3. Owain Glyn Dwr (in 1400).

4. Keir Hardie (in 1900).

5. 'Foreigners' (used from about AD 780 for people living west of Offa's Dyke).

6. W. H. Davies (it was an account of his life on the road and in dosshouses, published in 1908).

7. Aberfan (in 1966).

8. Plaid Cymru ('Party of Wales', founded in 1925).

9. Lawn tennis (his patent is dated 1874).

10. Merthyr Tydfil (in 1804; the locomotive pulled heavy weights a distance of nine miles).

124 MARRIAGE

1. Walter Sickert (in 1913).

2. Mr Rochester (in Charlotte's Brontë's *Jane Eyre*, published in 1847).

3. Rembrandt (in 1634).

4. Baseball star Joe Dimaggio (in 1954; she married James Dougherty in 1942 and Arthur Miller in 1956).

5. The future emperor Justinian (married Theodora in AD 525 and became Byzantine emperor two years later).

6. Franz Liszt (Cosima was Wagner's second wife; they married in 1870).

7. Adolf Hitler and Eva Braun (in Hitler's underground bunker, on the day before the couple committed suicide).

8. Martin Luther (in 1525).

9. Mozart's *The Marriage of Figaro* (in 1934).

10. Jeff Koons (in 1991, but their marriage broke up in 1992; under her real name, Ilona Staller, she is also an active politician in Italy).

125 RUSSIA

1. Kiev (from about 1030).

2. That they should deprive Stalin of power (Lenin's third stroke, in 1923, prevented him contacting anyone in a position to act on his instruction).

3. Leo Tolstoy (after wandering from his home in midwinter in 1910).

4. They were Viking tribes (established in Russia from about AD 825).

5. The KGB (Cheka was the acronym of the organization established by Lenin in 1917 to suppress political dissent).

6. Vice-president Richard Nixon and Soviet leader Nikita Khrushchev (in 1959).

7. Russia and Ukraine (in 1991).

8. Alexander Pushkin (he fought the duel with Georges d'Anthès in 1837).

9. Fyodor Dostoevsky (the novel was published in 1862).

10. Boris Yeltsin (the coup was against Mikhail Gorbachev, who was on holiday in the Crimea).

1. The samurai (from about 1200).

2. Karaoke (developed in Japan in about 1965; '*kara*' means 'empty' and '*oke*' is an abbreviation of '*okesutora*', the word for 'orchestra').

3. *Sei-i-tai-shōgun*, or shogun (in 1192).

4. The message that they must accept defeat in the Second World War (in his first ever radio broadcast, in August 1945).

5. *I-go*, known in the West as 'go' (traditionally introduced in AD 735).

6. The Anti-Comintern Pact (agreed in 1936 against the USSR).

7. The potter Bernard Leach (in 1911).

8. Manchuria (occupied in 1931 and renamed Manchukuo by the Japanese in 1932).

9. Hokusai (the earliest of these colour-printed woodcuts was published in 1830).

10. '*Ukiyo-e*', or the 'floating world' (from about 1650; Japan's popular theatre, the kabuki, was one of these entertainments).

127 SETTLED IN LONDON

1. Henry James (remained in London until 1898, when hc moved to Lamb House in Rye).

2. Berthold Lubetkin.

3. Karl Marx.

4. Marie Rambert (the school is now known as the Rambert School of Ballet and Contemporary Dance).

5. Johann Christian Bach.

6. John Singer Sargent.

7. George Frederick Handel.

8. Gordon Selfridge (opened Selfridge's in 1909).

9. Jacob Epstein.

10. Anna Pavlova.

1. Sonja Henie (in 1928, 1932 and 1936).

2. The PLO and Israel, or Yasser Arafat and Yitzhak Rabin (the Accords were agreed in Oslo and signed in Washington in 1993).

3. The Swedish tennis player Björn Borg (1976–80 inclusive).

4. The Battle of Copenhagen (in 1801; he did so in order to avoid seeing the signal to withdraw from the vicinity of Copenhagen's harbour).

5. Gustavus III (assassinated at a midnight masquerade in 1792; the event inspired *Un Ballo in Maschera*, first performed in 1859).

6. Denmark (*c.* AD 960).

7. By strangulation (he was a prehistoric victim, found in Tollund Moss in Denmark in 1950 with part of the noose still round his neck).

8. The Vasa dynasty in Sweden.

9. The Norwegian explorer Fridtjof Nansen (in 1893; he had to abandon the *Fram* in 1894, continuing with sledges and dogs and one companion).

10. Niels Bohr (in 1913).

129 ARCHITECTS

1. The Guggenheim Museum in Bilbao.

2. Sports arenas for the Berlin Olympics.

3. In the courtyard of the Louvre in Paris (it was completed in 1993).

4. The Bauhaus.

5. The Parthenon in Athens (construction began in 447 BC).

6. Frank Lloyd Wright (in 1935).

7. Deutscher Werkbund.

8. The World Trade Center (construction began in 1966 – it was destroyed in 2001 by the 9/11 attack on its twin towers).

9. Vienna (it was completed in 1910).

10. Edinburgh's New Town.

130 EGYPT

1. Upper and Lower Egypt (*c.* 3100 BC).

2. Anwar el-Sadat and Menachem Begin, the leaders of Egypt and Israel (for their Camp David peace treaty of the same year).

3. Gamal Abdel Nasser (in 1952).

4. Syria (in 1958 – they went their separate ways again in 1961).

5. It was found at a village in Egypt known variously as Rashid or Rosetta (by a contingent of Napoleon's soldiers, in 1799).

6. Saladin (bringing Egypt back to Sunni orthodoxy, in 1171).

7. The discovery of the tomb of Tutankhamun (in 1922).

8. Abu Simbel (*c.* 1250 BC).

9. Ptolemy, one of Alexander the Great's generals (in about 323 BC).

10. Cairo (in 1811).

131 FIRST ON THE CASE

1. Edgar Allan Poe (Dupin features in *The Murders in the Rue Morgue* (1841), now considered to be the first detective story).

2. *The Big Sleep* (Raymond Chandler's first novel, published in 1939).

3. Hercule Poirot (in Agatha Christie's novel, published in 1920).

4. Adam Dalgliesh (in P. D. James's *Cover Her Face*).

5. Father Brown (in *The Innocence of Father Brown* (1911), by G. K. Chesterton).

6. *Casino Royale* (Ian Fleming's first novel, published in 1953).

7. Lord Peter Wimsey (in the 1923 novel by Dorothy L. Sayers).

8. Inspector Maigret, or Commissaire Jules Maigret (in the first novel that Georges Simenon published under his own name, in 1931).

9. Sam Spade (in Dashiell Hammett's novel, published in 1930).

10. Miss Marple (Jane Marple, the second of Agatha Christie's famous detectives; she first appeared in 1930, ten years after Hercule Poirot).

132 SEVEN

1. *The House of the Seven Gables* (published in 1851; there was a tradition in Hawthorne's family that an ancestor had been cursed when serving as a judge in the Salem witchcraft trials of 1692).

2. *Seven Samurai* (1954).

3. Old Sarum (the most notorious of the rotten boroughs, when the Reform Bill was first put before Parliament).

4. American cyclist Lance Armstrong (in 2005).

5. Denmark and Sweden (the war began in 1563).

6. *The Leningrad Symphony* (because he completed it during the siege of Leningrad; it was first performed in Kuibishev in 1942).

7. Seven (in about AD 700; the word 'heptarchy' derives from the Greek for 'rule by seven').

8. Walt Disney's *Snow White and the Seven Dwarfs* (1937).

9. They were all prostitutes (murdered in 1888).

10. Robert E. Lee (opposing a Union army led by George B. McClellan, in 1862).

133 FRANCE

1. *A Bout de souffle* (*Breathless*; 1960).

2. Henry IV, the king of France (in 1610).

3. Pierre Boulez (established the Institut de Recherche et Coordination Acoustique/Musique in 1976).

4. Talleyrand (Charles Maurice de Talleyrand-Périgord; he became an abbot in 1775).

5. In Paris in the 1790s (during the French Revolution, in 1792).

6. Astérix (written by René Goscinny and drawn by Albert Uderzo; first appeared in 1959).

7. Jean-Antoine Watteau; he painted *L'Enseigne de Gersaint* (*The Shop Sign of Gersaint*) in 1721.

8. *La Comédie humaine* (*The Human Comedy*; published from 1842).

9. Django Reinhardt and Stéphane Grappelli (in 1934).

10. Antoine-Laurent de Lavoisier (in 1794).

134 ROBERT

1. *Nanook of the North* (1922).

2. St Giles' Cathedral in Edinburgh (the chapel was completed in 1911).

3. Oil drops (the 'oil-drop experiment' of 1909, in which tiny charged droplets of oil were suspended between two metal electrodes).

4. *The Ragged Trousered Philanthropists* (1914).

5. 'Blowin' in the Wind' (written by Dylan in 1962 and featured in this album of 1963; it had been released as a single by Peter, Paul and Mary earlier in 1963).

6. New Lanark (from 1800).

7. The Indochina War (the war fought by the Vietminh against the French; Capa was killed by a landmine in the year of the French defeat, 1954).

8. Proxima Centauri (discovered in 1915).

9. 'Do They Know It's Christmas?' (1984).

10. Tam o' Shanter (the poem of that name was published in 1791).

135 CAVE

1. At Altamira (in 1879).

2. *Homo sapiens* (anatomically modern humans, living about 90,000 years ago).

3. Ellora (the caves were created from about 1000).

4. The Essenes (*c.* AD 68).

5. In Phoenix Park (in 1882).

6. Edith Cavell (in 1915).

7. Dunhuang, or Tun-huang (the caves date from about AD 650).

8. Henry Cavendish (1766).

9. Fingal's Cave (his concert overture *The Hebrides (Fingal's Cave)* was premiered at Covent Garden in 1832).

10. Chauvet Cave (dating from about 28,000 years ago; it was discovered in 1994).

136 DISCOVERIES

1. The electron (in 1897).

2. The True Cross (the cross on which Christ died; Helena supposedly discovered it when she visited the city in about AD 327).

3. Nuclear fission (with its predictable possible consequence – a bomb of massive power).

4. The 'bee space' (in 1851; he discovered the amount of space that bees best like between cones in a hive).

5. The barometer (he discovered in 1643 that changes in atmospheric pressure are reflected in changes of level in a column of mercury).

6. Cosmic background radiation (earlier predicted to be a necessary result of the Big Bang and discovered in 1964).

7. The bacillus that causes tuberculosis (*Mycobacterium tuberculosis*, discovered in 1851).

8. Nimrud (in 1845).

9. The capillaries, carrying blood from arteries to veins (observed in 1661, thus verifying William Harvey's theory of circulation).

10. Blood groups (he classified the ABO system in 1901).

137 BOY

1. He is said to have picked up the ball and run with it during a football match at Rugby School in 1823 (but there is no contemporary evidence of this).

2. The cowpox virus (in 1796, after he observed that milkmaids who had had cowpox seemed not to be susceptible to smallpox).

3. *Brokeback Mountain* (2005).

4. Robert Frost (the book was published in 1913).

5. The Beastie Boys (the album was released in 1986).

6. *Homo erectus* (the skeleton was found in 1984 near Lake Turkana by Kamoya Kimeu, in Richard Leakey's team).

7. Vikram Seth (the novel was published in 1993).

8. The boyars, members of Russia's most privileged aristocratic families (in 1698).

9. *Black Boy* (published in 1945).

10. Christian boys, taken from their families to become slaves in the personal service of the Turkish sultan (from about 1450).

138 IRAN

1. Bam (more than 40,000 people died, in 2003).

2. The *Shah-nama* (meaning 'book of kings', completed in about 1010).

3. The US embassy in Tehran (in 1979).

4. At Persepolis (work began in 518 BC).

5. The Pahlavi dynasty (in 1925).

6. Zoroaster (*c.* 580 BC).

7. They were Mongols (descendants of Genghis Khan).

8. Painting (working in about 1500, he painted in a style of lively realism that greatly influenced the later Mughal school in India).

9. Mohammed Mossadegh (in 1953, after he had nationalized Britain's oil assets in the region in 1951).

10. Aga Khan (in 1818).

139 POETRY

1. The west wind ('Ode to the West Wind' was written mainly in a wood near Florence and published in 1820).

2. Gerard Manley Hopkins (from about 1876).

3. Emily Dickinson (she died in 1886; the six volumes were published between 1890 and 1936).

4. 'If' (published in 1910).

5. *Piers Plowman* (written in about 1367).

6. The Mersey (they were three of the group known as the Liverpool Poets; they published *The Mersey Sound* in 1967).

7. Dante (describing the new poetry of northern Italy, *c.* 1260).

8. *Leaves of Grass* (which had been issued in nine ever-enlarging editions by the time of Whitman's death in 1892).

9. 'Jerusalem' (published in 1804).

10. *Beowulf* (Heaney's translation was published in 1999).

140 SIX

1. The Iroquois League (known as the Six Nations after 1722).

2. Catherine of Aragon (the first of Henry VIII's six wives; of her six children, only Mary, born in 1516, crowned in 1553, survived beyond infancy).

3. The Sistine Choir (along with the Sistine Chapel, in 1471).

4. The Golan Heights (in 1967).

5. Frederick II (in 1228).

6. The Bugs Moran gang (in Chicago in 1929, massacred by followers of Al Capone).

7. The Han dynasty (the stones were inscribed in about AD 175).

8. In France (The Six – in French *Les Six* – a group formed in 1920 by Georges Auric, Louis Durey, Arthur Honegger, Darius Milhaud, Francis Poulenc and Germaine Tailleferre).

9. Harry Vardon (he won in 1896, 1898, 1899, 1903, 1911 and 1914).

10. Tolpuddle, in Dorset (they were the Tolpuddle Martyrs, transported in 1834 as a result of anti-union legislation).

141 GERMANY

1. Nuremberg (Nuremberg Eggs, about three inches in diameter and worn usually on a ribbon round the neck, were first made in about 1500).

2. '*Blut und Eisen*', meaning 'blood and iron' (he first used the phrase in 1862).

3. Philipp Melanchthon (joined the university in 1518).

4. Richard Strauss (his opera *Salome* was first performed in 1905).

5. The *Minnesinger* (from about 1250).

6. Joseph von Fraunhofer (in 1817 he observed in the solar spectrum more than 500 dark lines, now often referred to as Fraunhofer lines).

7. Berlin (*Goodbye to Berlin* was published in 1939; Isherwood had lived in Berlin from 1929 to 1933).

8. At Leipzig (with the Allies inflicting a heavy and almost unprecedented defeat on Napoleon, in 1813).

9. Immanuel Kant (*The Critique of Pure Reason* was published in 1781).

10. Sans Souci (construction began in 1746).

1. Toussaint L'Ouverture (arrested in 1802 after concluding a treaty with the French; he died in 1803).

2. Burke and Wills (Robert O'Hara Burke and William John Wills).

3. Evelyn Waugh (in *A Handful of Dust*, published in 1934).

4. Albert Camus (the novel, usually known in English as *The Outsider*, was published in 1942).

5. Alfred Tennyson, in 'The Charge of the Light Brigade' (the poem was published within six weeks of this event in the Crimean War).

6. Philippe Pétain (defended Verdun in 1916 but was convicted of treason in 1945).

7. Napoleon declared himself emperor (in 1804, causing Beethoven to change the name of his new symphony from *Bonaparte* to *Eroica*).

8. The Ku Klux Klan (the novel was published in 1905).

9. *La Chanson de Roland* (*c*. 1130).

10. Alexander Portnoy (in *Portnoy's Complaint*, published in 1969).

143 INVENTIONS

1. Thomas Edison (it opened in 1876).

2. A steam wagon (probably the first working mechanical vehicle, in 1769 – the first locomotive on rails was Richard Trevithick's, in 1804).

3. The mouse.

4. Paper (in AD 105).

5. Humphry Davy (the Davy lamp was in use from 1815).

6. He created the first pair of contact lenses (in 1887).

7. Samuel Morse (his version was capable of transmitting messages over much longer distances than previously).

8. The microscope (in 1590 – the telescope is also a Dutch invention, by Hans Lippershey in 1608).

9. Computing (much more powerful than earlier versions, the Electronic Numerical Integrator And Computer was completed in 1946 at the University of Pennsylvania).

10. Salisbury Cathedral (the clock was installed in 1386 and tells the time only by striking the hours).

1. Basra (now in Iraq, then part of the Ottoman empire).

2. Israel (Ariel Sharon was prime minister from 2001 to 2006).

3. He was leading the Third Crusade (in 1190).

4. Abraham (in Genesis; if historical, probably around 1800 BC).

5. The Young Turks (Jön Turkler in Turkish).

6. Greece (invaded in 1919, successfully resisted by Turkish troops led by Mustafa Kemal Atatürk).

7. They were all caliphs and all assassinated (Omar, the second caliph, died in AD 644; Othman, the third caliph, died in AD 656; Ali, the fourth caliph, died in AD 661).

8. Palestine (the organization was set up in 1920 to protect Jewish settlements in Palestine, part of which became the state of Israel in 1948).

9. Sumer (from about 3100 BC).

10. Portugal (in 1514).

145 TWO

1. Vermont and Kentucky (joined the Union in 1791 and 1792 respectively; the stars were added in 1795).

2. Judah and Benjamin (after the Assyrian disaster in 722 BC).

3. Henri Matisse (in 1910).

4. Julius Caesar (in 55 and 54 BC).

5. Richard Henry Dana (the book was published in 1840).

6. Westminster Abbey (the funeral of Edward the Confessor and the coronations of Harold II and William I, all in 1066).

7. Benjamin Disraeli ('one-nation Conservatism' is a central theme in his 1844 novel *Coningsby*).

8. The number of presidential terms for which anyone could be elected.

9. Sweden (*c.* 1720).

10. England and Scotland (by the Act of Union, a century after the union of the crowns when James VI of Scotland became also James I of England in 1603).

146 BOOK

1. The Granth, the holy book of Sikhism (named in 1704).

2. Rip Van Winkle.

3. The ration book.

4. Thomas Cranmer (it was first published in 1549).

5. Daoism (the title in Chinese is *Daodejing*, *c.* 400 BC).

6. Marcus Aurelius (he began writing the books in about AD 170).

7. In Alexandria (it was written in Greek in about 300 BC, when he was teaching in the famous museum there).

8. The Sentimental Bloke (he featured first in the poems and then in a film of 1919).

9. *Old Possum's Book of Practical Cats* (Old Possum was much assisted by T. S. Eliot, in 1939).

10. *A Potter's Book* (1940).

147 ITALY

1. Giuseppe Mazzini (attempting to promote insurrection, in 1831).

2. The bones of St Mark (the pork would discourage the Muslim officials in Egypt from inspecting the barrel, in about AD 828).

3. Giuseppe Garibaldi (in 1860, to win control of the island for the king in waiting, Victor Emmanuel II; red shirts were worn almost as a uniform by his followers).

4. Opera.

5. Count Galeazzo Ciano (appointed foreign minister by Benito Mussolini in 1936 and executed after the Verona trials in 1944).

6. The ability to play *piano* (soft) and *forte* (loud) (added by the Florentine harpsichord maker Bartolomeo Cristofori, in 1698).

7. Venice (in 1470).

8. Vittorio de Sica (in 1948).

9. In Milan Cathedral, as the king of Italy (in 1804 he had had himself crowned emperor of France in Notre-Dame).

10. John Keats (in 1821; Shelley was drowned in the Gulf of Spezia a year later).

1. *The Farewell Symphony* (performed at Esterházy in 1772, when the annual return to Vienna was long overdue).

2. Sergei Rachmaninov (his *Rhapsody on a Theme of Paganini* was written beside Lake Lucerne in 1934).

3. *Façade* (she spoke the words of her poems to his musical settings).

4. Dmitri Shostakovich (in 1936, on Stalin's orders).

5. Ravi Shankar (in 1971).

6. *Turandot* (Puccini died in 1924).

7. Yehudi Menuhin (in 1924).

8. Kathleen Ferrier (in 1943).

9. Alexander Scriabin (from 1905).

10. Karlheinz Stockhausen (in 1957).

149 SEVEN

1. The Anti-Corn Law League (the Corn Laws were repealed in 1846).

2. *Scott of the Antarctic* (1948; the 1952 symphony has the title *Sinfonia Antartica*).

3. The Seven Years War (in 1756).

4. Mark Spitz (in 1972).

5. The Holy Roman Emperor (under a system established by Charles IV in 1356).

6. The Seventh Day Adventists (after holding a General Conference in Battle Creek, Michigan, in 1863).

7. The seven known planets, which at that time included the sun and the moon (their names provided the days of the week in about AD 50).

8. The Austin Seven, which also became known as the Baby Austin.

9. *The Seventh Seal.*

10. The Confederate States of America (in 1861, at the start of the American Civil War).

150 JOHN

1. The Falkland Islands (in honour of Viscount Falkland, in 1690).

2. Dorelia (he first met her in 1902).

3. The collected plays of Shakespeare (this edition of 1623 is now known as the First Folio).

4. 'In Flanders Fields' (written, in 1915; McRae was a Canadian army surgeon).

5. *Big Brother* (first broadcast in 1999).

6. Ship money, to Charles I (in 1636; the tax was supposed to be levied only when there was a specific danger to England's coastal towns).

7. That the spread of cholera was due to infected water in the pump (in 1854).

8. The MJQ, or Modern Jazz Quartet (in 1952).

9. Teaching evolution (in the Scopes Monkey Trial of 1925).

10. Sierra Leone (ousting the civilian president, Ahmad Kabbah, in 1997).

151 ECONOMICS

1. The Continental System (imposed in 1806 to prevent British ships entering any continental port).

2. Maastricht (in 1991; the euro became currency on 1 January 1999).

3. John Maynard Keynes (the book was published in 1919).

4. *Mrs Thatcher* (the book was published in 1983).

5. Florence (in 1345).

6. Bretton Woods (during the Bretton Woods Conference held in 1944).

7. *Small is Beautiful* (1973).

8. '. . . a new deal for the American people' (in 1932 – and the policies of his first term became known as the New Deal).

9. Ephesus (the coins were made of a naturally occurring alloy of gold and silver and were struck with a distinguishing mark on one side, from about 650 BC).

10. Wall Street (in 1817).

152 VICTORY AND DEFEAT

1. American Carl Lewis (for the 100m, 200m, 4x100m relay and the long jump).

2. It was the carriage in which the armistice had been signed after the defeat of Germany in 1918.

3. Muslims, or Arabs (defeated by Charles Martel in AD 752).

4. Anatoly Karpov (in the world chess championship of 1985).

5. The Swiss halberd (able to jab, grapple and slash).

6. The Ottoman Turks (giving them control of Serbia).

7. At Isandhlwana in South Africa, immediately before a minor but better-known British success at Rorke's Drift in the Anglo-Zulu War.

8. Leopoldo Galtieri (the Argentinian leader resigned three days after the Falklands defeat and subsequently served five years in prison).

9. Imran Khan.

10. Jimmy Connors.

153 MICHAEL

1. Michael Faraday (reported his discovery of the first law in 1832).

2. Michael Jackson (the album was released in 1982).

3. Michael Ondaatje (the novel was published in 1991, the film released in 1996).

4. Michael Holroyd (the volumes were published in 1967 and 1968).

5. Michael Rysbrack (in 1731).

6. Michael Howard (in 2005).

7. Michael Cardew (in 1926).

8. Michael Frayn (the play was first produced in 1998).

9. Michael Caine (in 1966).

10. Michael Tippett (in 1941).

1. Edwin Landseer (knighted in 1850).

2. Ivan Pavlov (at a congress in Madrid in 1903).

3. The Pony Express (in 1860).

4. Rabbit (first introduced in Updike's 1960 novel, *Rabbit, Run*).

5. New Zealand and/or Australia (he was a New Zealand gelding that had a prodigiously successful career in Australia after winning the Melbourne Cup in 1930).

6. Operation Sea Lion (in 1940).

7. The caves at Ajanta (in 1817).

8. Georges Cuvier (introducing scientific palaeontology, in 1812).

9. Horse (*All the Pretty Horses* was published in 1992).

10. The Tiger Moth (designed in 1931).

155 MEALS

1. Oliver Wendell Holmes (it was published in 1858).
2. Theodoric, leader of the Ostrogoths (in AD 493).
3. *Naked Lunch* (published in Paris, in 1959).
4. Myra Hess (from 1939).
5. The Eucharist (established in about AD 31).
6. Peter Paul Rubens (in 1636).
7. The Tea Ceremony (from about 1300).
8. Holly Golightly (the book was published in 1958).
9. Alexander the Great (in 323 BC).
10. William McKinley (winning a second term in 1900).

1. The Aztecs (moving south from northern Mexico from about 1150).

2. Alexandria (*c.* 280 BC).

3. The Oregon Trail (established in 1843).

4. Semitic (from Shem, one of Noah's three sons in Genesis; they moved north in about 3000 BC).

5. Ireland (after the Great Famine of 1845).

6. Aryans (migrated in about 1500 BC).

7. The *Empire Windrush* (arrived from Jamaica in 1948).

8. The Philistines (migrated in about 1200 BC).

9. Northern Italy (the Cimbri were defeated by the Romans in 101 BC).

10. They were Vikings ('Norman' is derived from 'northman'; their leader, Rollo the Ganger, was granted feudal rights in Normandy in AD 911).

157 KNOWN AS

1. Lord Haw-Haw (he was hanged as a traitor, for his broadcasts from Germany, in 1946).

2. Because they met in a Jacobin convent (from 1789).

3. Parsees (meaning 'Persians', from about AD 900).

4. Robert Campin (he was painting in about 1430).

5. Angry Young Men (from about 1955).

6. The Stockholm Bloodbath (1520).

7. The Axis powers (from 1936).

8. Archimedes (supposedly designed the Archimedes Screw in about 250 BC).

9. Lollards (from about 1400).

10. Roman and italic (developed in about 1495).

158 STONE

1. The Olmecs (*c.* 1000 BC).

2. Samuel Pepys (who celebrated his survival of the operation on its anniversary every year).

3. New York (the commission came from the proprietor of the *New York Herald* in 1869).

4. Jean-François Champollion (in 1822).

5. The Marquee Club, 165 Oxford Street (in 1962).

6. Osip Mandelstam.

7. A curling stone (used in the Scottish equivalent of bowls, played on ice).

8. *All Quiet on the Western Front* (based on the novel by Erich Maria Remarque).

9. Julius II (with the architect, Donato Bramante, in 1506).

10. Skara Brae (a neolithic village dating from about 2500 BC).

159 FIRSTS IN LITERATURE

1. Soames Forsyte (in *The Man of Property* by John Galsworthy, published in 1906; the completed series was published in 1922 as *The Forsyte Saga*).

2. R. K. Narayan (the novel was published in 1935).

3. Katherine Mansfield (the collection was published in 1911).

4. *Tarzan of the Apes* (1914).

5. Magic realism (Borges's novel was published in 1935).

6. Uncle Remus (in a story in the *Atlanta Constitution* in 1879).

7. *Oroonoko* (1688).

8. It was the first novel to deal openly with a lesbian subject.

9. Richard Hannay (the novel was published in 1915).

10. Margaret Atwood.

160 FOUR

1. John Harrison (the final and winning version was tested in 1761).

2. The Scottish Colourists (Francis Cadell, Samuel Peploe, Leslie Hunter and John Duncan Fergusson; their exhibition was in 1924).

3. The first four-minute mile was run on this track in Oxford by Roger Bannister (in 1954).

4. Frank Harris (the volumes were published between 1920 and 1927).

5. Richard Strauss (*Four Last Songs* was performed in 1950).

6. *Le Grand Meaulnes* (completed in 1913).

7. Gautama Buddha (at Sarnath in about 424 BC).

8. 'Dr Livingstone, I presume' (uttered when he found Livingstone at Ujiji, in modern Tanzania, in 1871).

9. Gutzon Borglum (he began work in 1927 on the heads of George Washington, Thomas Jefferson, Abraham Lincoln and Theodore Roosevelt).

10. Katharine Hepburn (in 1933).

161 PETER

1. Petrograd (he changed it from St Petersburg, because that sounded too German).

2. *Pierrot Lunaire* (1912).

3. Creating German colonies in Africa (from 1884, beginning the 'scramble for Africa').

4. *The Boy Who Wouldn't Grow Up* (*Peter Pan, or the Boy Who Wouldn't Grow Up* was first produced in London in 1904).

5. He bought the island of Manhattan from local Indians (and called it New Amsterdam, in 1626).

6. Peter Handke (in 1966).

7. As a crusader (he led the largest of the popular groups from Germany on the First Crusade, in 1096).

8. Peter Jackson (the first was released in 2001, the others in 2002 and 2003).

9. Pop artist Peter Blake (in 1967).

10. Pierre Laval (Vichy prime minister, in 1945; Vichy head of state Philippe Pétain was also sentenced to death but Charles de Gaulle commuted his sentence).

1. All Jews who would not convert to Christianity (in 1492, when the Christian reconquest of Spain was completed by the capture of Granada).

2. Isaac Albéniz (the series was completed in 1909).

3. El Cid (from the Arabic '*sayyid*', meaning 'chief' or 'lord'; he captured Valencia in 1094).

4. Severiano Ballesteros.

5. St Ignatius of Loyola (whose leg was shattered when he was defending Pamplona and who went on to found the Society of Jesus, or the Jesuits).

6. Luis Buñuel (the film was released in 1972).

7. Ferdinand and Isabella (in 1469).

8. Federico García Lorca (in 1936).

9. Andrés Segovia.

10. The court painter Diego Velázquez (in 1656; in *Las Meninas* the royal couple are seen in a mirror on the far wall).

163 GOLD

1. The Cheltenham Gold Cup.

2. *On Golden Pond.*

3. *Das Rheingold*, by Richard Wagner (the introduction to his four-opera cycle *Der Ring des Nibelungen*, and the first to be staged).

4. The *Golden Hind* (returned to England in 1580).

5. Barry Goldwater (in 1964 – Johnson did not stand for re-election in 1968).

6. Golda Meir (in 1974).

7. The Golden Temple, in Amritsar (in 1984 – this was the main reason for her assassination by members of her Sikh bodyguard later that year).

8. *The Golden Bough* (1890).

9. Carlo Goldoni (from about 1740).

10. Erich Korngold.

164 MODERN ASSASSINATIONS

1. Italy (the king was Humbert I, or Umberto I).

2. William McKinley.

3. Aung San.

4. Mahatma Gandhi.

5. Iraq (in 1958).

6. Hendrik Verwoerd.

7. Robert Kennedy (in the Ambassador Hotel in 1968).

8. Anwar el-Sadat (because of his peace agreement with Israel).

9. Laurent Kabila.

10. Pim Fortuyn.

165 PEOPLES

1. The Magyars (from AD 895).

2. Scythians (mummified bodies, together with carpets and felt artefacts, have been discovered from 1949).

3. The Visigoths (driven north after the first Muslims arrived in AD 711).

4. Mayan (Thompson was the US consul in Mexico and began his archaeological work there in 1904).

5. The Vandals (captured Carthage in AD 439).

6. Africa (the San and the Hottentots are surviving members of the group today).

7. The Beaker people (arrived in Britain in about 2000 BC and are named after the characteristic drinking vessels found in their tombs).

8. New Mexico (in the 1680 uprising the Indians killed twenty-one missionaries and some 400 colonists).

9. The Mongol tribes (he was elected in 1206 and took the name Genghis Khan).

10. The Seljuk Turks (their leader, Togrul Beg, became sultan of Baghdad in 1055; the Ottoman Turks came to prominence later, in the thirteenth century).

166 GEORGE

1. The Railway King (from 1844).

2. Gershwin (George was the composer, Ira the lyricist; the first of their joint musicals was *The Passing Show of 1916*).

3. Jean-Antoine Houdon (in 1785).

4. Civilians (the medal was created by George VI in the second year of the Second World War).

5. Phlogiston (in 1702 – the search for this elusive, and in fact non-existent, substance was prominent in eighteenth-century science).

6. Sinclair Lewis (in his novel *Babbitt*, published in 1922).

7. Madras (in 1644).

8. *Trilby* (1894).

9. Martin Luther (in 1522, after being outlawed at the Edict of Worms).

10. Prince Albert (the Albert Memorial, designed and constructed from 1863, was opened in Kensington Gardens by Queen Victoria in 1872).

167 WEAPONS

1. The longbow (one of its earliest appearances).

2. Doodlebug (the V-1 Flying Bomb began falling on London in 1944; '*Vergeltungswaffe*' means 'retaliation weapon' in German).

3. Alamagordo (in 1945).

4. The flintlock (the spark that ignites the gunpowder is provided by a flint; it was introduced in France in 1610).

5. Evelyn Waugh (the first of the trilogy, *Men at Arms*, was published in 1952).

6. Clara Bow (in 1927).

7. Amy Lowell (in 1914).

8. The crossbow (from about 250 BC).

9. The Sex Pistols (the first punk rockers).

10. The catapult (lobbing great stones at enemy fortresses from about 340 BC).

168 SPORT AFTER 1900

1. Gordon Richards.

2. British driver Lewis Hamilton (in 2007; he won in Canada and then in the USA in his sixth and seventh races).

3. Ice hockey (in the Canadian National Hockey League in 1945).

4. Rod Laver.

5. Stoke City, the two dates being 1931 and 1964 (in the middle section of his long career he played for Blackpool, from 1947 to 1961).

6. Mike Tyson (in 1986).

7. Daley Thompson.

8. Billy Wright (he made his 100th appearance in the national team in 1959 and went on to achieve a total of 105 caps).

9. Lester Piggott (he won for the first time in 1954, when he was only eighteen; the last of his nine wins was in 1983).

10. Baseball (combining teams from the National League and the American League).

169 AUSTRALIA

1. The First Fleet (which carried about 750 convicts).

2. Douglas Jardine (in 1932; Jardine devised the policy of aiming at the body of the batsman in the hope of a catch, and Harold Larwood bowled the most controversial deliveries).

3. Ned Kelly's gang (in *The Story of the Kelly Gang*, released in 1906).

4. Evonne Goolagong (she had a second Wimbledon win in 1980 and a total of fourteen Grand Slam victories).

5. The Australian Gold Rush (in 1851).

6. Cathy Freeman.

7. Henry Handel Richardson (the book was published in 1917).

8. Patrick White (in 1973).

9. Edna Everage (created by Barry Humphries in 1955, later to become Dame Edna, superstar).

10. 100 (tantalizingly just under, at 99.94 runs, when he retired in 1948).

170 THEATRE

1. *Le Barbier de Séville*, or *The Barber of Seville* (in 1775).

2. Donald Wolfit (the play was first performed in 1983).

3. Jean Racine.

4. The Berliner Ensemble (in 1949).

5. At Oberammergau (in 1634; the play is now performed every ten years).

6. Laurence Olivier (in *The Entertainer*, in 1957).

7. Thespis (winner of a drama competition in Athens in 534 BC and considered to be the first actor – as a result, all actors are thespians).

8. In Canterbury Cathedral, where the murder of Thomas Becket had taken place in 1170 (the play was first performed in 1935).

9. *The Crucible*, set at the time of the Salem witchcraft trials of 1692 (and first performed in 1953).

10. *West Side Story* (in 1957; they were composer, choreographer and lyricist).

171 KNOWN AS

1. The *Pathétique*, or *Pathetic* (it premiered in 1893).

2. The Netherlands, under Spanish rule (a reign of terror was introduced by the regent, the duke of Alba, in 1567).

3. *Fijnschilder*, or 'fine painters' (*c.* 1640).

4. Hologram (the creation of a three-dimensional image from reflected light was first achieved in 1947).

5. Puerto Rico, in the town of Lares (the name 'Grito de Lares', meaning the 'Cry of Lares', is in a tradition deriving from the 'Grito de Dolores' uprising in Mexico in 1810).

6. Neo-Platonism (Plotinus moved from Alexandria to Rome in about AD 244).

7. Demotic (meaning 'for the people' in Greek, developed in about 700 BC).

8. The Vulgate (translated in about AD 405 and later considered to be for the common people ('*vulgus*'), of whom more knew Latin than Hebrew or Greek).

9. The Immortals (*c.* 500 BC).

10. Caesarion (when he was born in 47 BC, she said he was the son of Caesar, and Caesar accepted him as such).

1. Hurling (the Irish Hurling Union was formed in 1879).

2. The Irish Free State (in 1922; it became Eire in 1937 and the Republic of Ireland in 1949).

3. The Orange Society (formed to resist Irish nationalism, in 1795).

4. Countess Constance Markiewicz (in 1918).

5. Brian Boru (in 1014, when he was seventy-three).

6. Riverdance (after it was performed in the Eurovision Song Contest in 1994).

7. At Drogheda (during his Irish campaign, in 1649).

8. They met – previously unheard of for a prime minister of Northern Ireland and a *taoiseach* of the Republic (they had two meetings in 1965).

9. Sinn Féin (Irish for 'we ourselves', in 1902).

10. The occupation by republicans of the General Post Office building in Dublin (in 1916).

173 JOHN

1. John and Charles Wesley (the club was the beginning of Methodism, in about 1730).

2. John Winthrop (he began his journal in 1630).

3. 'Sea Fever' ('I must down to the seas again, to the lonely sea and the sky . . .'; the collection was published in 1902).

4. The Silver Beatles (in 1960 – soon shortened to something more memorable).

5. Johnny Weissmuller (in 1932).

6. John Franklin (in 1845).

7. John Kenneth Galbraith (in 1958).

8. Gough Whitlam (in 1975).

9. A Christmas card (in 1843).

10. A flush toilet (the pamphlet was printed in 1596).

1. Carbon dioxide (he called it 'fixed air', in 1754).

2. Alfred Nobel (creating dynamite, in 1867).

3. Mauve, or 'aniline purple' (the name Perkin gave it, in 1856).

4. Thalidomide (taken from about 1956 by pregnant women in nearly fifty countries and shown in 1961 to be the cause of a massive disaster).

5. Hydrogen and helium (about 13.7 billion years ago).

6. Radiocarbon dating (in the USA in 1949).

7. Gunpowder (in about 1040).

8. Isotope (coined in 1913 to describe anomalies in the periodic table).

9. Gas (in 1648; he derived it from the Greek word for 'chaos').

10. The oral contraceptive (developed by Syntex in 1951).

175 MARY

1. Mary Shelley (*Frankenstein, or the Modern Prometheus* was published in 1818).

2. Mary Quant (in 1966).

3. Mary Anning (in 1811).

4. Maryland (the land was granted to Lord Baltimore in 1632).

5. Mary Seacole (established her own 'British Hotel' for the purpose in 1855, during the Crimean War).

6. Mary Baker Eddy (in 1875; it was later considered the textbook of Christian Science).

7. The Marylebone Cricket Club (the arbiter of everything to do with cricket, in 1864).

8. Lady Mary Wortley Montagu (the treatment was dangerous because it involved infection from a smallpox pustule instead of the later use of a vaccine derived from the cowpox virus).

9. The Maryinsky Company (Bronislava joined it in 1908).

10. Mary Jo Kopechne (she was a passenger in the car that Edward Kennedy accidentally drove off a bridge and into a deep channel in 1969).

176 HOLY

1. Albert Schweitzer (with his wife, in 1913).

2. Hinduism (the texts were written from about 400 BC, from a much earlier oral tradition).

3. *Ben Hur* (1880).

4. Amritsar (*c.* 1590).

5. Laurence Sterne (in *Tristram Shandy*, the first part of which was published in 1759).

6. Buddhism (*c.* 250 BC).

7. Vatican City (in 1929).

8. The Ming dynasty (the temple was built in about 1425).

9. The crossbow (at the Second Lateran Council, in 1139).

10. Desmond Tutu (appointed in 1986).

177 THE UNITED STATES

1. Galveston (more than 8000 people died).

2. Take a census of the population (every ten years).

3. The Great Awakening (*c.* 1735).

4. Ernest Hemingway (in 1961).

5. The 'domino theory' (coined in 1954).

6. Chicago.

7. The Sioux (in 1890).

8. To George III (from the Second Continental Congress in Philadelphia, in a final bid for peace).

9. Monticello (the Italian for 'mound', because he was building it on a hilltop in Charlottesville).

10. The Pacific (they reached it in 1805 and were back in St Louis in 1806).

178 SHIPS AND BOATS

1. Ironclad ships (in 1862, during the American Civil War).

2. They were sunk by a Japanese air attack (off the coast of Malaya, two days after Pearl Harbor, in December 1941).

3. The tsar Peter the Great (in 1697, to discover what was needed to create a Russian navy).

4. To attack Athens (in 490 BC, during the Greco-Persian Wars).

5. Cadiz (in 1587 – a daring exploit that became known in England as 'singeing the king of Spain's beard').

6. Commodore Matthew Perry.

7. John Knox (in 1547).

8. Liberty ships (the first, the *Patrick Henry*, was launched in 1941).

9. *Steamboat Willie* (1928).

10. Toulon (after Hitler invaded Vichy France, in 1942).

179 PAUL

1. Friedrich Paulus (thus saving the lives of the remaining German Sixth Army, in 1943).

2. Jean-Paul Sartre (*L'Etre et le néant*, in French, was published in 1943).

3. Paul Hindemith (in 1923).

4. Concord, in Massachusetts (he was one of several riders carrying news of imminent British attack in 1775, but he was arrested between Lexington and Concord).

5. Paul Dirac (in 1930).

6. Paul VI (he was elected pope in 1963).

7. Paul Allen (in 1975).

8. Charlotte Corday (who stabbed him in his bath in 1793).

9. Paul Scofield (in 1960).

10. Paul Kruger (in 1897).

180 FLIGHT

1. The fruit fly (*Drosophila melanogaster*, in 1910).

2. *The Flying Dutchman* (in Dresden in 1843).

3. The governor flicking at the consul with his fly whisk (in 1827).

4. *The Flies* (*Les Mouches*; written in 1943).

5. *Flying Down to Rio* (1933).

6. The Flight of the Earls.

7. *Lord of the Flies*, by William Golding (published in 1954).

8. *Papillons*, or *Butterflies* (published in 1832).

9. The Flying Doctor Service (launched in Australia in 1928).

10. The flying shuttle (in 1733; it speeded up weaving).

181 TRAVEL

1. She was the first steamship to cross the Atlantic (completing the journey in nineteen days).

2. The Comet (designed by de Havilland, went into service with BOAC in 1949).

3. The first transcontinental railway in the USA (the Union Pacific and the Central Pacific railroads met there).

4. John McAdam (it was the first of a great many macadamized roads and was completed in 1815).

5. The hovercraft (designed by Christopher Cockerell, it crossed the Channel in 1959).

6. The opening of the Suez Canal (in 1869).

7. The Via Appia (completed in 312 BC).

8. The North Sea and the Baltic (the canal opened in 1832).

9. The Mini (designed by Alec Issigonis for the British Motor Corporation).

10. Underground railway (steam trains ran between Paddington and Farringdon Street from 1863).

182 ENGLAND

1. Cavaliers and Roundheads (used by parliamentarians of the royalists and vice versa, from about 1641).

2. The English oratorio (*Esther* was first performed in 1732).

3. The king's veto of Catholic emancipation (in 1801).

4. Whist (*A Short Treatise on the Game of Whist*).

5. Jeremy Bentham (his book *Principles* was published in 1789).

6. The young Queen Victoria (she refused in 1839 to dismiss politically committed ladies of her bedchamber).

7. The Stock Exchange (in 1773).

8. To Holland, or the Netherlands (in 1608, to avoid the religious restrictions imposed on them in England).

9. Elizabeth I (in Spenser's epic poem *The Faerie Queene*, of which the first three books appeared in 1590 and the other three in 1596).

10. Russia (the charter was granted to the Muscovy Company in 1555).

183 ROBERT

1. Robert the Bruce (according to legend, he was encouraged by the perseverance of a spider to continue his fight for the Scottish crown, in 1306).

2. Robert Schumann (in 1854).

3. David Roberts (published the lithographs in six volumes, completed in 1849).

4. Robert Peel (in 1842, at a level of 7 pence in the pound).

5. Robert Graves (the book was published in 1929).

6. Robert Emmet (in 1803).

7. Robert Helpmann (in 1948).

8. The Reverend Robert Walker (in 1792; the painting is now in the National Gallery of Scotland).

9. Robert Adam (in 1757).

10. Robert Boyle (the relationship was defined by him in 1662 and subsequently became known as Boyle's Law).

184 SUN

1. 25 December (in AD 274, long before a date was established for Christmas Day).

2. Robert Redford (and Paul Newman played Butch Cassidy, in the 1969 film *Butch Cassidy and the Sundance Kid*).

3. Sun Yat-sen (in China in 1910).

4. Sunset Boulevard (in 1911).

5. That the earth is in orbit round the sun (a theory put forward by Aristarchus in about 270 BC).

6. Giovanni Domenico Cassini (working at the Paris Royal Observatory, in 1672; his estimate was 87 million miles, instead of 93 million miles).

7. Tax fraud (he is the founder of the Unification Church, convicted in 1982).

8. St Petersburg.

9. Dublin (the day began with targeted assassinations by the IRA and ended with security forces opening fire on a crowd at a football match).

10. Derry, or Londonderry, in Northern Ireland (when British troops opened fire on a civil rights march).

185 WEALTH

1. In Texas (near Beaumont, in 1901).

2. *The Wealth of Nations* (its full title is *An Inquiry into the Nature and Causes of the Wealth of Nations*; it was published in 1776).

3. Rubber (in about 1900).

4. The Copper Belt (from mineral discoveries in 1909).

5. Croesus (king of Lydia in about 550 BC and best known now in the phrase 'as rich as Croesus').

6. *The Theory of the Leisure Class* (1899).

7. YouTube (launched in February 2005, bought by Google in October 2006).

8. The largest uncut diamond yet discovered (the Cullinan Diamond, found in 1905 and cut as two gems, both now in the British Crown Jewels).

9. The US industrialist Andrew Carnegie (the book was published in 1889).

10. Eduardo Paolozzi (the sculpture was installed in 1993).

186 KNOWN AS

1. Synthetic cubism (from about 1913).

2. Muhammad, from Mecca to Medina (in AD 622 – '*hegira*' is usually translated as 'emigration' or 'flight').

3. The Rumble in the Jungle (fought in 1974; Muhammad Ali regained his title).

4. Domenikos Theotokopoulos (born in Crete, moved to Spain in 1577).

5. The Golden Horde (from 1237).

6. The Sicilian Vespers (1281).

7. 'Baby Doc' (from 1971, when he succeeded his father, François 'Papa Doc' Duvalier, as president of Haiti).

8. The Second Triumvirate (in 43 BC – the First Triumvirate was Julius Caesar, Pompey and Crassus in 60 BC).

9. Pangaea ('all earth' in Greek, formed about 250 million years ago).

10. Art, mainly conceptual (they came to prominence in 1988 in an exhibition called 'Young British Artists' organized by Damien Hirst).

187 AFRICA

1. Kenya (in 1921).

2. Lucy (when the partial skeleton was discovered, in Ethiopia in 1974, 'Lucy in the Sky with Diamonds' was on the radio).

3. The slave trade (transporting slaves north to the Arab world, which stretched at the time from Spain to Persia).

4. Jan Smuts, in 1939 (he was prime minister 1919–24 and 1939–48).

5. Great Zimbabwe.

6. Ken Saro-Wiwa (in 1995).

7. Soweto (from about 1950).

8. Moise Tshombe (in 1960).

9. Seretse Khama, because he had married a white British woman, Ruth Williams (they were married in 1948; he was banned from return in 1950).

10. Bernard Montgomery.

188 THE FIRST MILLENNIUM

1. Boudicca, or Boadicea (made a devastating attack on Roman soldiers and civilians in Colchester in AD 60).

2. Mecca (from around AD 100; the idols were housed in the Ka'ba).

3. Roman socks (in tombs dating from about AD 250).

4. Christianity's New Testament (for which many rival texts were considered for inclusion; the document was distributed in AD 367).

5. Attila (in AD 445).

6. Venice (the islands were first settled by fugitives in AD 569).

7. The Archangel Gabriel (who dictated to him the words of Allah in about AD 613).

8. Japan (the empress commissioned in AD 768 a million copies of a Buddhist charm for distribution to pilgrims).

9. Vikings (from Norway, in AD 838).

10. Greenland (*c.* AD 981).

189 FIRST YEARS OF CENTURIES

1. Iceland (Vikings had settled on the island from AD 874).

2. Henry I (on the death of his brother William II).

3. The Cathars (also known as the Albigensians, because they were wrongly considered to be particularly strong in the town of Albi).

4. Holy Year, or Jubilee (proclaimed as such by Pope Boniface VIII, with plenary indulgences for pilgrims who made their way to Rome).

5. *Meistersinger*, or 'master singers'.

6. On the coast of what became Brazil (Brazil was therefore Portuguese while almost all the rest of Central and South America was Spanish).

7. Oratorio (the work, *La Rappresentazione di Anima e di Corpo*, was something like a concert performance of a religious opera).

8. France (he left everything to a grandson of Louis XIV, provoking the War of the Spanish Succession that lasted from 1701 to 1714).

9. At Marengo (in northern Italy, in June, after coming through the St Bernard Pass in May).

10. *The Dream of Gerontius* (Newman's poem was published in book form in 1866).

190 1900s

1. Mercedes (Mercedes Jellinek was the daughter of their investor and distributor Emil Jellinek).

2. *Buddenbrooks*.

3. Pepsi-Cola.

4. *The Riddle of the Sands*.

5. Helen Keller (her autobiography, *The Story of My Life*, had been published the previous year).

6. The Russian battleship *Potemkin* (thousands died after troops fired on a resulting demonstration).

7. Genetics (the word 'genetic' had been used before, but Bateson coined the plural as a form akin to 'politics').

8. Russia (building on the Entente Cordiale of 1904 between Britain and France).

9. Fyodor Chaliapin (the success of this venture encouraged Diaghilev to present his first season of ballet in Paris in the following year).

10. The body louse (he discovered that lice carry the bacteria of epidemic typhus; endemic typhus is similarly spread by fleas).

191 1910s

1. Gustav Mahler (at the premiere of his own *Symphony No. 8*).

2. David Lloyd George (his National Insurance Bill affected only workers in a few selected industries).

3. Ludwig Wittgenstein.

4. Ulster, or Northern Ireland (provoking in response, later that year, the formation of the Irish National Volunteers in the south).

5. Vorticism (a new movement in British art).

6. Pyrex.

7. The Spartacus League (named after the Roman gladiator and rebel).

8. The convoy system (protection in numbers).

9. The Marne (in the second battle of the Marne; in July and August, the Allies pushed back the final German advance on the Western Front).

10. The Hall of Mirrors, or Galerie des Glaces, in Versailles (the room where the German empire was proclaimed in 1871, after the defeat of France).

192 1920s

1. Cary Grant, then Archibald Leach (he moved to Hollywood in 1931 and there changed his name).

2. A British airship (it burst into flames on its fourth flight, in 1921, and crashed into the Humber).

3. *Ulysses* by James Joyce (not published by any mainstream publisher until the Random House edition of 1934).

4. The Ruhr (Germany's industrial heartland, occupied on the grounds that Germany was defaulting on the reparations due to France).

5. The Marx Brothers (in *I'll Say She Is*; at this stage, Gummo was part of the group and Zeppo had not yet joined).

6. Enigma (used by the Germans in the Second World War and deciphered in Britain from 1941).

7. *Seven Pillars of Wisdom*, by T. E. Lawrence (describing the Arab uprising of 1917).

8. Clarice Cliff (when she was twenty-eight).

9. Henry Moore (the commission for the relief *West Wind* on the exterior of the London Underground headquarters).

10. Tintin (*Tintin in the Land of the Soviets* was the first comic strip by Hergé to feature the young reporter).

193 1930s

1. Decency in the movies (also known as the Production Code, it was introduced by Will H. Hays, chairman of the Motion Picture Association).

2. Irgun (carried out clandestine operations until the creation of the independent state of Israel in 1948).

3. Éamon de Valéra (he remained Ireland's leader until Fianna Fáil lost the election of 1948).

4. Engelbert Dollfuss (he was assassinated by Austrian Nazis in the following year).

5. The photographer Leni Riefenstahl.

6. *Lulu*.

7. Salvador Dalí (it was a Surrealist exhibition, in London).

8. The Krebs cycle, or citric acid cycle (biochemical reactions in cells leading to the release of energy were discovered by Krebs with Albert Szent-György).

9. *Scoop*.

10. *It's That Man Again* (starring Tommy Handley and running until his death in 1949).

194 1940s

1. The bus (Chamberlain assured the House of Commons, on 5 April 1940, that Hitler 'has missed the bus' – because of the Phoney War delay).

2. Crete (they had driven the same British force out of mainland Greece shortly before).

3. Vidkun Quisling (founder of the Norwegian Fascist Party, and President of Norway till his arrest in May 1945).

4. Zoot suits (the Zoot Suit Riots erupted in Los Angeles between zoot suiters and sailors on leave).

5. General Frank Merrill (the US press gave them the nickname Merrill's Marauders).

6. May (Victory in Europe Day was 8 May 1945; V-J Day, or Victory over Japan Day, could not be celebrated until 15 August).

7. He said that an iron curtain had descended across the continent.

8. The Polaroid camera (Polaroid was the name of Land's firm; first demonstrated in February 1947, the camera was on the market by Christmas 1948).

9. Benjamin Britten and Peter Pears (the Aldeburgh Festival has been held each June since then in the Suffolk seaside town).

10. Simone de Beauvoir (the French title is *Le Deuxième Sexe*).

195 1950s

1. Julius and Ethel Rosenberg (they were convicted in 1951 of passing nuclear secrets to the USSR and executed in 1953).

2. Henri Matisse.

3. DNA (her photographs helped James Crick and Francis Watson to discover the structure of the DNA molecule in 1953).

4. *On the Waterfront.*

5. Graham Sutherland (the portrait was subsequently destroyed by Churchill's widow).

6. Glenn Gould.

7. The marriage of Ted Hughes and Sylvia Plath.

8. The 'sack' (essentially somewhat shapeless).

9. Brendan Behan.

10. Solomon Bandaranaike.

196 1960s

1. At Sharpeville, near Johannesburg.

2. Adolf Eichmann (tried in Jerusalem and sentenced to death).

3. A Wal-Mart Discount store (the number of stores in the USA alone has grown to more than 1000 by 2007).

4. Sexual intercourse (in his poem 'Annus Mirabilis').

5. Freddie Truman (in a match at the Oval).

6. He was the first man to walk in space (he moved around outside the *Voshkod 2* spacecraft for more than ten minutes).

7. Che Guevara (he was captured in Bolivia in the following year and executed).

8. *The Graduate.*

9. American Indians (AIM stands for the American Indian Movement).

10. To attend the Woodstock Music Festival.

197 1970s

1. *M*A*S*H* (the TV series ran from 1972).

2. *A Clockwork Orange* (starring Malcolm McDowell).

3. Syphilis (the Tuskegee Syphilis Experiment, in Alabama, had studied 399 African Americans from 1932 to 1972 without treating their syphilis).

4. Jack Lynch.

5. Scott Joplin (whose music had become famous in the previous year from the score of the film *The Sting*).

6. David Hockney.

7. Carl Andre (the artwork was bought in 1972 but the controversy only erupted in 1976).

8. Jacques Chirac (then leader of a recently formed neo-Gaullist party).

9. Andrew Motion (appointed Poet Laureate in 1999).

10. The future of Southern Rhodesia (which became independent as Zimbabwe the following year).

1. Archbishop Oscar Romero.

2. Deng Xiaoping (though he never held an official post as head of state or government).

3. As the lead character in the film *Tootsie*.

4. The compact disc.

5. Nicaragua (to destabilize the Sandinista regime).

6. Oprah Winfrey (the *Oprah Winfrey Show*, or *Oprah*, is commissioned up to 2011).

7. Jean-Claude 'Baby Doc' Duvalier.

8. Steffi Graf.

9. Pan Am (the wreckage of Pan Am Flight 103 fell on Lockerbie).

10. The Velvet Revolution.

199 1990s

1. Tim Berners-Lee, working at CERN in Geneva.

2. Alan Bennett.

3. Rodney King (riots erupted in the city as a result).

4. Pablo Escobar.

5. Alexander Solzhenitsyn.

6. Fermat's Last Theorem (a theorem which Pierre de Fermat said he had proved, in a note found after his death in 1665, but without further explanation).

7. Creutzfeldt-Jacob Disease (linked to BSE but capable of infecting humans).

8. 'Candle in the Wind' (at the funeral of Diana, Princess of Wales, on 6 September 1997).

9. Khartoum (it turned out that it was a pharmaceutical factory and that the US evidence was flawed).

10. The impeachment of President Bill Clinton (the charges were perjury and obstruction of justice, relating to the Monica Lewinsky affair).

200 THE NEW MILLENNIUM

1. Rap artist Eminem.

2. Anthrax.

3. Wikipedia.

4. Hamid Karzai (the office became fully his two years later, when he won Afghanistan's presidential election).

5. Eduard Shevardnadze.

6. SARS (Severe Acute Respiratory Syndrome, reported in 2003 but declared 'eradicated' by the World Health Organization in 2005).

7. Leonardo DiCaprio.

8. Iranian president Mahmoud Ahmadinejad said this of Israel.

9. Montenegro.

10. Ian Paisley (of the Democratic Unionist Party) and Gerry Adams (of Sinn Féin), planning for the Northern Ireland Assembly formally reconvened in May 2007.

Acknowledgements

It is a great pleasure, after a long career as a writer, to find myself at last with a penguin on my spine. For this I have to thank Georgina Laycock, who heads the Penguin reference section. She asked me in April of this year whether I would write a book of quiz questions. Oddly enough, nobody had ever suggested that before, in the forty-five years since I asked my first question on the airwaves. In addition to commissioning the book, Georgina has been a rich source of excellent ideas – in particular the linking themes, as half-hidden clues to likely answers within each set of questions, and the delightful vignettes that decorate each page and add another, often elusive, hint as to the topic in question. I am also grateful to Diana Baring, who has been my agent from the start and who emerged from a peaceful retirement to take up the cudgels once more on my behalf.

Later, in the very rushed process of creating the book, I was lucky to have an exceptionally hawk-eyed editor, Emma Horton. It has been the first time that I have published a book in the internet age, and it was strange to discover that one no longer needs to meet one's editor for those long sessions over an office table. In what I imagine it must be like to play poker with unseen opponents on the web, I have engaged with Emma in a passionate but always good-humoured series of email tussles on such vital issues as capitalization and commas.

Looking back over many years, this is also a good occasion to thank my colleagues at Granada who kept *University Challenge* up and running during the twenty-five years of my time in the chair. In particular, I am grateful to two men, both sadly now dead. Douglas Terry was my genial producer for about fifteen years. But the real heart of the production team was my friend Peter Mullings, director of the show for almost my entire time with it and doubling as the producer for several years at the end. I never ceased to marvel at his unfailing professionalism and commitment to the programme.

And I cannot possibly end without a word of thanks to the many thousands of students who were bright enough and brave enough to play the game – nearly all of whom expect me to remember them, and most of whom, alas, are in that respect disappointed.